NATHALIE SPENCER

GOOD MONEY

UNDERSTAND YOUR CHOICES.
BOOST YOUR FINANCIAL
WELLBEING.

WHITE LION
PUBLISHING

Brimming with creative inspiration, how-to projects and useful information to enrich your everyday life, Quarto Knows is a favourite destination for those pursuing their interests and passions. Visit our site and dig deeper with our books into your area of interest: Quarto Creates, Quarto Cooks, Quarto Homes, Quarto Lives, Quarto Drives, Quarto Explores, Quarto Gifts or Quarto Kids.

First published in 2018 by White Lion Publishing
an imprint of The Quarto Group
The Old Brewery, 6 Blundell Street
London N7 9BH
United Kingdom

www.QuartoKnows.com

A catalogue record for this book is available from the British Library.

ISBN 978 1 78131 757 0
Ebook ISBN 978 1 78131 782 2
10 9 8 7 6 5 4 3 2 1
2022 2021 2020 2019 2018

Designed and illustrated by Stuart Tolley of Transmission Design

Printed in China by Toppan Leefung Printing Ltd

CONTENTS

INTRODUCTION

Money touches our lives in innumerable ways. On a basic level it is a necessary instrument, which we exchange for goods and services to help us survive. Yet it is also much more than that. For better or worse, money is a measuring stick, often used to convey status to others and sometimes to reassure worth to ourselves. We use it to buy things we need (food and shelter) and things we certainly don't (diamond-encrusted cars). Money can pay for things or experiences that bring us joy, yet can also be a source of tension, stress and worry. So what does it mean to be good with money?

Financial wellbeing is about making ends meet day to day, planning for the long term and being prepared for inevitable hiccups along the way. Being good with money is not simply knowing about various financial products (although that is useful), it is about our behaviour and the decisions we make regarding how we spend, save and make our money work for us. There are various aspects of our human psychology that influence how we manage money, and learning more about their interplay can help us to make better decisions.

If you're currently feeling the pinch, you're not alone. Research finds that many people struggle when it comes to money. This is not just the case for those of us on low incomes; people can have a high salary and still find

it hard to manage their money well. By one estimate, 1 in 5 people across Europe find it difficult to pay their rent or mortgage each month. Most people have less than three months' worth of income saved up, and 1 person in 3 has no savings at all. This leaves people vulnerable when 'life happens' – the boiler breaks, your parent gets ill, you lose your job. Without any financial slack it is harder to juggle multiple priorities.

Of course, there is more to life than just wealth. While money isn't everything, and certainly doesn't guarantee happiness, there are some important benefits to improving your financial wellbeing. Building up wealth provides against such nasty surprises and opens up choices that may otherwise be unavailable. In this sense, financial wellbeing can be somewhat self-reinforcing, with low financial wellbeing creating further difficulties and high financial wellbeing creating further opportunities.

In the following pages we'll learn why our behaviour with money isn't always straightforward, and doesn't always follow the guidelines set out in a traditional economics textbook. A textbook approach often assumes that people are highly numerate, love spreadsheets, deliberate over every decision and have impeccable willpower. The reality is that, for most of us, this isn't an accurate reflection. We are

By better understanding human nature, we can improve our own personal decision-making to avoid the downward tug of financial fragility and move toward the upward spiral of financial wellbeing.

human, with our human psychology and human cognition. Often, we can get by just fine. But sometimes our behaviour is self-defeating, such as when the feeling that you really *ought* to get a handle on your debt is met with an equally powerful avoidance to check how much is actually owed. In these cases we'll learn some ways to help ourselves change course. The aim is that, by better understanding human nature, we can improve our own personal decision-making to avoid the downward tug of financial fragility and move toward the upward spiral of financial wellbeing, recognizing bad money traps and developing good money practices.

In Part 1, we'll reflect on the many different 'ways of being' with money, how money can change a situation, and uncover why there seems to be unrelenting pressures and demands on us to strive for better, more or bigger, rooted in our evolutionary psychology and reinforced by societal norms.

Parts 2, 3 and 4 explore intriguing habits of mind and patterns of behaviour that create potholes on the road to financial wellbeing. This road takes us from making ends meet (day to day, month to month, year to year), to building a buffer for those unexpected dips in income or spikes in expenditure, and to planning for the long term so that we have choices and comfort tomorrow and beyond.

In part 5 we'll discuss some approaches to stay on track, and point to some ways we can spend wisely, keeping both our financial and general wellbeing in mind.

There is no magic formula to follow on these pages that will instantly make you rich. There isn't even any specific personalized advice of the type you might get from talking with a financial adviser, poring over the details of your own incomings and outgoings. The ideas presented here, grounded in decades of behavioural science research, draw on many different features of human nature to help explain some of our idiosyncrasies with money, and in so doing, may help you on to the path towards 'good money'.

HOW TO USE THIS BOOK

This book is organized into 5 parts and 20 key lessons covering the most intriguing ideas from behavioural science and personal finance today.

Each lesson introduces you to an important concept,

and explains how you can apply what you've learned to everyday life.

As you go through the book, TOOLKITS help you keep track of what you've learned so far.

Specially curated FURTHER LEARNING notes give you a nudge in the right direction for those things that most captured your imagination.

At BUILD+BECOME we believe in building knowledge that helps you navigate your world. So, dip in, take it step-by-step or digest it all in one go – however you choose to read this book, enjoy and get thinking.

WHAT DOES
TO BE GOOD
MONEY?

IT MEAN
WITH

MONEY AND US

LESSONS

The way we are with money is the product of both very personal values and experiences, and the specifics of the situation.

Money isn't just a transactional instrument to be exchanged for goods and services. The way we come about money and what we do with it are so deeply personal that it would be naive to believe anything but the claim that money matters beyond keeping us materially comfortable. It matters a lot.

How do we get money? Maybe we earn our money via a job that we love (or one that we hate), or have received an inheritance from someone we cherished. Perhaps it's the product of some smart investments, or maybe we are financially supported by someone else. What we choose to do with the money we have to some extent reflects who we are, our expectations and our values.

In the first lessons, we'll learn that the way we are with money is the product of many things, including our personality, our past experiences and the symbolism we attach to it, to name just a few. Is wealth a vehicle for power? Autonomy? Choice? Even love? Perhaps all of the above. Looking way back into our evolutionary past, we learn that some of the pressures we feel around accumulating and displaying wealth may be rooted in a deep-seated motivation to be desirable enough to build a family.

And while we might not recognize these pressures in exactly the same way today, we tend to believe that certain things will bring us happiness, or that a particular path in life will bring fulfilment. Researchers have found that our predictions in this arena aren't always accurate – we can be bad forecasters, though we don't always recognize it – and this can make it difficult to know with any certainty what to strive for.

In addition, our complex relationship with money means that when money is introduced into a situation, it changes the nature of it, and can turn a social interaction into a market transaction with altogether different properties, and sometimes with surprising consequences. Let's begin . . .

MONEY MATTERS

You know the moment. The one where, all of a sudden, you realize that the person next to you, who you thought you knew so well, is absolutely, totally, utterly different from you when it comes to money. It might be a friend, a relative, even a partner, yet it feels, in that instant, as though they are from a different planet. 'You paid *what* for that?!'; 'What are you so worried about, live a little!'; 'Are you sure you can afford that?'; or even 'Stop buying me stuff!'

When we talk about money, we are talking about so much more than its transactional value. There are innumerable 'ways of being' with money – from the extent to which we get pleasure from it or are pained by spending it, to its symbolic value and the meaning we take from it, to how we manage it (or don't).

For example, the terms 'tightwad' and 'spendthrift' might not sound very scientific,

but actually they feature in a body of research into the pleasure and pain we feel when spending money. In 2008, Scott Rick and his colleagues from the University of Michigan developed a scale to measure whether people identified as finding it too painful to spend money ('tightwads'), not painful enough ('spendthrifts') or somewhere in an unconflicted middle ground. While the majority of people studied are unconflicted, 1 in 5 identify as a tightwad, and similarly roughly 1 in 5 as a spendthrift.

Having tightwad tendencies is not quite the same as being frugal. Frugality is characterized by finding pleasure in saving and thrift, whereas tightwads find it painful to part with money, so often go without spending on something that, on reflection, they would have liked to have had.

Are you partnered to someone on the other end of the spectrum? You're not alone.

Perhaps unsurprisingly, Rick and colleagues found that these mixed relationships tend to have more disagreements over money matters. Tightwad couples tend to have a better financial position than spendthrift couples, with mixed partnerships falling somewhere in between.

Of course, this isn't the only categorization when it comes to our attitudes towards money. What about meaning – what do we see reflected in what money brings to us, beyond the material goods that it can buy? A group of researchers in the UK surveyed over 100,000 people about what money means to them. For some people, money seems to represent love, a way to show affection through material generosity. For others, it means power, a way to realize status or control. Others view it as *security*. And finally, for some, money represents *autonomy* – it enables freedom.

In most studies, it seems that attitudes towards money are largely independent of income or education level. But they do appear to be correlated with the likelihood of experiencing an adverse financial event, such as going overdrawn, being denied credit or even having a car repossessed: those who associate money with power are more likely than others to have experienced one of these events, whereas those who associate money with security are less likely. It is important to note that with these studies we learn only about association, and not about causality. So it might be the case that experiencing one of these events shapes your money attitude, not the other way around.

CONTEXT MATTERS

How are you with money? What does it mean to you? What features in your life so far seem to shape how you relate to money now?

It is a good idea to examine your own way of thinking about money, and the choices you make. Feel like one of the descriptions on the previous page suits you well? You may find some comfort in knowing that there are other people who think the same way. But don't get caught up in labels: just because you might relate more to A than B in many situations, doesn't mean that you always will, and it certainly doesn't mean that you have to.

Context shapes our decision landscape. The country you live in influences how much you'll spend on healthcare and housing or how much you save for retirement. Culture

and language affect the mental models through which we make sense of the world. The job you have will dictate your earnings. Childhood experiences can plant seeds for attitudes that appear later in life, surfacing at times of adversity.

For example, Vladas Griskevicius and colleagues found that, when facing a time of scarcity such as a recession, people who

grew up with less financial means tended to behave more impulsively, preferring short-term rewards over waiting for a better return later on, as compared to people who grew up in a household from a higher socioeconomic bracket. These differences don't appear in times of plenty.

Of course, it's not just past experience that matters. Our current environment crucially influences our money decisions by setting the decision landscape, as we'll see in the rest of the book. Remember those tightwads? Reducing the 'pain of paying' (see Lesson 6) can systematically shift their spending behaviour. Simply highlighting that a cost is low by calling it a 'small $5 fee' increased the likelihood that a tightwad would purchase it, highlighting just how important the decision environment is when it comes to behaviour.

As we've seen, there is no single blueprint for how we are with money – it depends on many different factors. Reflecting on our own personal relationship with money can help us step back, take stock and work towards keeping what we are happy with, while making adjustments to those aspects that we want to see changed.

OUR DEEP PAST

Designer shoes, the fanciest cars, the biggest gems . . . why are these so attractive to us?

Imagine you are just about to go and buy a seriously flash car. The boot is too small, and the seats are so low that it isn't that easy to get in to. Sure it's impractical, but boy does it look great. Think of the heads you'll turn! Now imagine the same situation but there is no one else around. Nobody. Just you. A last person on earth scenario. What do you think about the purchase now? What's the point of a flash car if no one else can see it?

The thought experiment highlights the fact that much of what we buy is not just for its usefulness or beauty to ourselves, but for what it means to others. And much of this spending, it is argued, can be explained by the evolutionary psychology behind our human needs. Researchers such as Doug Kenrick, Vlad Griskevicius, Gad Saad and Geoffrey Miller, among others, claim that the urge to fulfil certain evolutionary goals can explain purchasing trends and the strong pull we sometimes feel around spending. These main goals are: to protect ourselves; to avoid disease; to make friends; to gain status within a group; to find (and keep) a romantic partner; and to care for our offspring and relatives. When any one of these 'fundamental social challenges', as they are sometimes described, are at the forefront of our mind, it can influence our spending behaviour.

Researchers differentiate 'fundamental social challenges' from more proximate drivers of behaviour. Both are insightful.
01. Proximate drivers are surface-level explanations for why we do something.
02. Fundamental ultimate drivers are the deeper-rooted reasons behind our actions.

This is an important distinction because if we look only at proximate motivations, some behaviour can seem paradoxical until we understand the ultimate motivation driving them. For example, if tempted to buy that flashy car, the proximate motivation might be that you like the soft leather interior, but the ultimate motivation could be that such a demonstration of wealth may impress a potential mate.

Of course we all have individual differences – diverse personalities, capabilities and experiences – so not everyone will respond in the same way or to the same extent to these challenges. And not everyone subscribes to the evolutionary drivers theory about consumption; there are numerous critiques of it, not least of which is that it is difficult to prove (or disprove). Nevertheless it is an interesting way to think about our own (over-)consumption.

ULTIMATE DRIVERS

The idea of signalling our 'fitness' (being good at each of the seven fundamental social challenges) means that we may be tempted to spend more than necessary, buying flashy items to impress potential mates or friends, or to feel that we belong within a particular group. In a sense, the more expensive and conspicuously over the top the product is, the more credible the signal is to others because it is harder to fake. And because flashiness is a relative concept, this can lead to more and more spending.

The ultimate drivers are said to influence how we spend our money. For example, when *self-protection* is top of mind we may be more willing to spend money on home alarms, locks and the police (through taxes) to keep ourselves safe. The sound of someone coughing nearby can activate the *disease avoidance* drive, encouraging introversion and avoiding busy places, so we might choose to stay at home rather than indulge in an expensive night on the town.

If the drive to *make friends and alliances* is invoked, Nicole Mead and colleagues found that people are more willing to spend money on products that demonstrate some sort of group affiliation (such as a university T-shirt) or on products that other people like, all

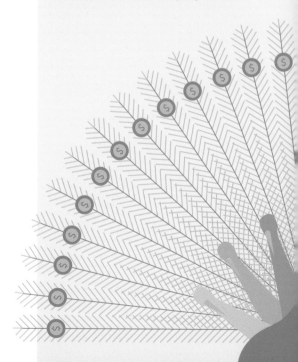

in the hope of being socially included. The drive to *gain status* may help explain ambition at work, and very conspicuous consumption of luxury goods to show off this status.

The *mate-acquisition, mate-retention* and *kin* care goals relate to successfully passing your genes on to the next generation. When trying to find a mate, people want to seem more attractive than their competition, so spending money on looking good is likely to occur. Once a match is made, the drive to keep the partnership strong explains why we place such value on anniversary gifts and other displays of affection. And finally, people invest time, energy and money in ensuring that their relatives have the best chance of a fulfilling future.

Of course, these ultimate drivers aren't always pulling in the same direction. Wanting to protect yourself would lead to conformity of behaviour (blending into a crowd, benefiting from safety in numbers), whereas when wanting to attract a mate, people want to stand out from the crowd. So by appealing to one goal over another, marketers can swing us to prefer a certain (potentially more expensive) good or service – or even to buy several different varieties of a product, each working towards fulfilling different evolutionary goals.

A little introspection could be useful to uncover some underlying drivers of spending. Why do you really want this product, given what you now know about these theories? What could be the proximate driver for your purchase; what could be the ultimate driver? Are you trying to signal something with this purchase, and if so, what?

To be clear, the answers to these questions don't necessarily point to a conclusion that you shouldn't buy it, simply that having reflected upon it you might decide that you don't want it after all, or maybe that you want something different instead.

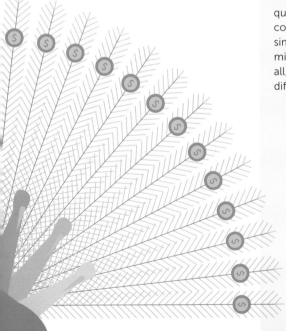

WHEN IT CO
MONEY, THE
CONTEXT M

MES TO
DECISION
ATTERS.

MISWANTING

'If only I had a bigger house, I would be happier.' Sounds reasonable enough, but is it really true? In general, we are not very good at predicting just how happy or unhappy certain circumstances will make us, and this matters because we may be using our money in ways that don't improve – or could even reduce – our wellbeing.

Generally speaking, people are good at predicting how an impending change will make them feel. That is, we are able to say that a night out with friends will make us feel good and a kick in the teeth will make us feel bad. What we are bad at is judging the importance of a single event and the duration of those future feelings.

FOCALISM

Focusing on one single event means that we fail to appreciate that other peripheral parts of our lives might be affected by the change. They could stay the same, or could become better or worse, in such a way that they counter the benefits or the drawbacks of the change. Or they may simply distract you from the effects of the focal event.

We also tend to underestimate the speed with which we can adapt. People are remarkably good at adapting to a change in circumstance – whether positive or negative. This is most famously illustrated in research from the 1970s by Philip Brickman and colleagues who found that over time lottery winners rate their happiness the same as non-winners. The researchers explain that adaptation to a new way of life after positive or negative events likely happens because the subsequent daily activities pale against the peak excitement of the life-changing event, and that we habituate to our new norm (see Lesson 17).

MISWANTING

Often we don't like or dislike a change as much as we thought we would have. If we're poor forecasters, who's to say that what we are striving for is the best change? We don't always get it right. University of Virginia and Harvard professors Tim Wilson and Dan Gilbert call this miswanting. Buying a bigger house might sound like a great idea – 'Imagine all the space! I'll be so happy!' – but fails to take into account that in the new house there will still be bills to pay and the difficult colleague at work. Pretty soon the bigger space just feels like a regular-sized space, and the happiness hit has worn off.

Many researchers try to uncover what does bring us happiness once we have 'enough' to cover the basics. The UN Sustainable Development Solutions Network (SDSN) finds that on a country level, indeed income matters, but so too do other important factors such as health (life expectancy), having someone to count on in times of trouble, generosity, freedom and trust in institutions. These factors influence our overall life satisfaction. When it comes to our daily moods, it has been reported that shorter commutes, spending time with friends, regular sex and fewer meetings with your boss make people happy. We'll learn in Lesson 20 some specific ways to get the biggest happiness bang for your buck.

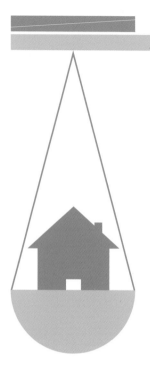

WARTS AND ALL

Correctly predicting how we will respond to changes in our situation is difficult, but there are ways in which we can try to do it better.

The problem of focalism, where we overemphasize the importance of one particular change to our life, can be helped by attempting to visualize the future, warts and all. Specifically, this is done by describing all the other things which would be part of our life in the future, not just the one change in question. Often, the quotidian aspects of our lives remain so – there will still be errands to run, laundry to do, spats with loved ones.

This approach worked when Wilson and his colleagues asked sports-fan students to predict how they would feel after their sports team won or lost an upcoming match. Half of the fans had also been asked to record the things they would likely be doing on the day of the game, such as studying, eating or socializing. This group, recognizing the peripheral events of the day, predicted that the match results would be less impactful than the other group predicted, and they were right.

Regarding the duration of our responses, keep in mind that, for better or worse, the effects of a one-off change may be short-lived. The fact that we become accustomed to changes in our situation doesn't mean that we should be reduced to fatalism or

For better or worse, the effects of a one-off change may be short-lived as we become accustomed to changes in our situation.

think that there's no point trying for that next promotion. But it does point to the need to carefully consider what type of life we are trying to create. Experiences, more than material goods, are anticipated and then held on to in your memory, so there is less likelihood of adapting and losing the joy. Nothing can compare to the remembered version of that special meal your mother made five years ago, or that Italian holiday last spring.

Moving house? Consider the trade-off between a bigger home further away and a shorter commute to work. Opting for a shorter commute should improve happiness in and of itself, but additionally, the extra time saved could be used to enjoy the other social activities that are found to improve our mood.

Finally, while having more and more money doesn't make us happier, having insufficient money can make us unhappy. When visualizing and planning your future it's important to build in a buffer of readily available savings for unexpected events.

PRICES, FINES AND INCENTIVES

Suppose you are a politician and you want people to change their behaviour – to start or stop doing something. Let's say you want people to stop climbing trees. What approach would you take to try to make this happen? You could ask people really nicely; you could use bans, making it illegal; you could even try to educate people – if only they knew the risks they would surely stop climbing!

Or you could use money, fining people for climbing trees. You might expect that to get someone to do more of something you should financially reward them, and to get someone to do less of something you should make it more costly. Indeed, this works in many situations, however, money isn't the only tool, or even the best tool, to motivate us or to influence our behaviour.

When money is introduced into a situation, it can turn what was a social interaction into a market transaction, sometimes with surprising knock-on effects. Behavioural scientists Uri Gneezy and Aldo Rustichini wanted to tackle the issue of people arriving late to collect their children from daycare. Over 20 weeks they studied the pickup patterns at 10 different daycare centres in Haifa, Israel. For the first few weeks they collected data to learn the frequency of late arrivals, then, in just over half of the centres, they introduced a financial penalty: parents were fined each time they collected late.

Surprisingly, the researchers found that late arrivals increased in the centres with the fine. Normally, in a social interaction, it is inconsiderate to the teachers if you collect late, so the cost to late parents is the guilt and embarrassment they feel at violating a social norm. But when the fine was introduced, parents were paying an actual price for their tardiness, thus absolving them of negative emotion, and the price was low enough that it was worth it for the extra flexibility.

So they stopped the fines. But the frequency of late arrivals did not return to the pre-fine levels. Perhaps parents no longer felt obliged to conform to the expected niceties of a social exchange. Or perhaps the fine provided the parents with new information: the low fine may have signalled that the cost to the daycare was also low, whereas before the parents couldn't really be sure. Whether or not the cost to the daycare actually was low is less relevant in this case than the parents' *interpretation* of that cost.

In a similar vein, offering people money to do things, especially when the activity is seen as socially important, can make them less likely to do it. Economists call this 'crowding out', when a financial perk cheapens the intrinsic feelings of social obligation, civic duty or even enjoyment or curiosity that we may have about doing something.

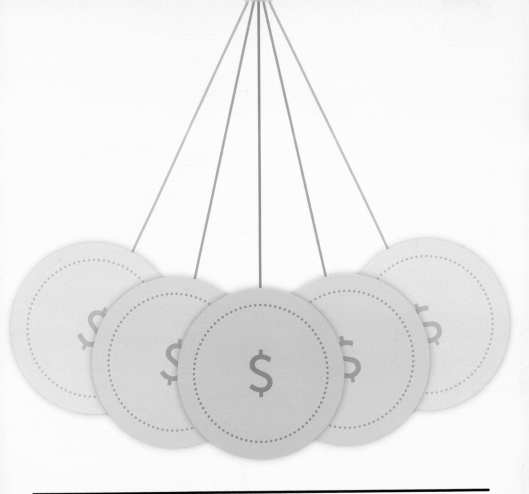

In Switzerland in 1997, a team of researchers wanted to gauge a region's appetite for allowing a nuclear power plant to be built in the vicinity. Although there were obvious downsides, when surveyed, more than half provided their approval. But when the inhabitants were told that they would be offered financial compensation if the plant were to be built, the approval rating plummeted to about 25%. For some, the compensation seemed to signal risk; after all, if you have to pay me to do something then maybe it is really risky or unpleasant. For others, the promise of financial compensation crowded out the sense of civic duty, the sense that although it wasn't necessarily welcomed it was the right thing to do.

THE PRICE OF PRICE TAGS

Rather than being purely profit-maximizing, when a situation is monetized people respond with a host of other considerations.

Research in this area is plentiful and finds that, alongside these crowding out and signalling effects, we also care about fairness, reciprocity and altruism. For example, Gneezy and Rustichini report that if people get paid very little for a task, they might do it worse than if they had been paid nothing at all; the payment makes it a market transaction, but the low value is seen as unfair. And when given a surprise financial bonus, people tend to reciprocate by putting more effort into the task at hand, at least initially.

So while it is undeniable that money – prices, fees, bonuses – plays a big role in influencing us, attaching money to a situation does not always ensure the outcome you may want or expect. Not everything should have a price tag. Pricing everything can lead us to miss out on more pleasant, efficient or fairer ways of being.

The nuclear power plant example shows that extrinsic, monetary rewards can squash pleasant feelings, for example, the pride of being a good citizen. So there is a hedonic rationale for omitting a price tag: without it, the activity might retain the intrinsic reward of a feel-good glow.

The daycare example illustrates that sometimes, the absence of talk about money allows the agreement or understanding between people to remain somewhat ambiguous. An 'incomplete contract' like this can benefit both parties when people generally work on the basis of mutual trust and cooperation. Setting fines introduced information, which in this case the parents used to the daycare's disadvantage.

But most importantly, when everything is priced, we have to ask what the implications are on fairness. Harvard professor Michael Sandel explores this topic in depth. From the trivial (paying to jump the queue at the airport) to the profound (paying for healthcare), more and more in life has a price attached to it. When this is the case, those who are rich can buy what they want to improve their quality of life, whereas the poor cannot, thereby further exacerbating inequality.

So, when thinking about how we work with colleagues, clients or suppliers, caring for family and socializing with friends, it could be worth reflecting on what incentives you are using with others, and what incentives are being used on you? When do we want these interactions to be priced and when do we not? We're often told to make a career from something we love, but consider how your affinity for a hobby could change once you start getting paid to do it.

TOOLKIT

01

How we are with money – how we feel, how easy or hard it is to spend, what it symbolizes to us – is shaped by so many different factors. Context matters; our past experiences and current environment shape our financial decisions. It is worth reflecting on the question: what does money mean to you?

02

Our desire to spend on different items is shaped by our evolutionary past, and some basic urges to impress other people, keep our family safe and take care of ourselves. This can manifest in some ways that seem puzzling: why spend so much money on a Ferrari when a Ford will get you from A to B just as well? Keeping the seven ultimate drivers of our behaviour in mind may help shed light on some of your own spending patterns.

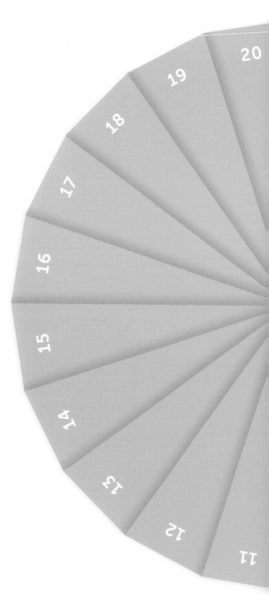

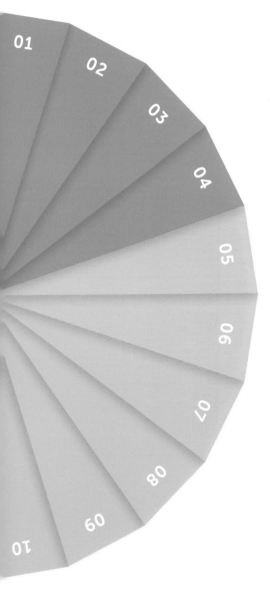

03

We are typically not very good at recognizing how emotionally resilient we are to changes in circumstance – whether positive or negative. Therefore we may end up 'miswanting' certain things and using money in ways that don't improve our financial, or general, wellbeing.

04

Money is one, but certainly not the only, tool to motivate behaviour. When money is introduced into a situation, it can change the way that we react, for example by 'crowding out' feelings of social obligation or a warm glow of doing something virtuous. We should question when pricing something serves our society well, and when it does not.

FURTHER LEARNING

READ

The Interdisciplinary Science of Consumption
Preston, S. D., Kringelbach, M. L., & Knutson, B. (Eds.) (MIT Press, 2014)
A collection of articles touching on many of the themes in part 1.

Rational Animal
Doug Kenrick and Vladas Griskevicius (Cambridge University Press, 2010)

When and why incentives (don't) work to modify behaviour
Gneezy, U., Meier, S., & Rey-Biel, P., *The Journal of Economic Perspectives*, 25(4), 191–209 (2011)

Miswanting: Some problems in the forecasting of future affective states.
Gilbert, D., & Wilson, T. in *Thinking and feeling: The role of affect in social cognition*, edited by Joseph P. Forgas, 178-197. (Cambridge: Cambridge University Press, 2000)

LISTEN

Everything you always wanted to know about money (but were afraid to ask)
Freakonomics podcast
freakonomics.com/podcast

WATCH

Why we shouldn't trust markets with our civic life
Michael Sandel
TED Talk

EXPLORE

Tightwads and Spendthrifts
Rick, S. I., Cryder, C. E., & Loewenstein, G. *Journal of Consumer Research*, 34(6), 767-782 (2008)
Check where you fall on the tightwad-spendthrift scale by answering the questions provided.

BBC Big Money Test
Learn more about money attitudes
bbc.co.uk/guides

MONEY IN THE DAY TO DAY

LESSONS

A key step towards improving financial wellbeing is to simply lift our head out of the sand.

One vital component of financial wellbeing is being able to make ends meet from payday to payday. From covering rent or mortgage, to groceries, clothing and entertainment, it is important to be able to pay for our everyday needs.

A first step in this stage is to get a clear picture of where our finances stand. In this section, we'll learn why it can be uncomfortable to dig into our bank statements to really begin to understand our financial position. And yet without this information, it is difficult – if not impossible – to determine how to best move forward. A key step towards improving financial wellbeing is therefore to simply lift our head out of the sand.

How does our environment, the way we pay for things and the way retailers market to us affect our spending?

Financial instruments have been changing at pace. No longer do we have to rely on cash and cheques; most of us now have access to a range of fancy new technologies to make payments nearly effortless. But what are the consequences of this newfound ease? Whereas with cash we had to physically hand over notes and coins, and therefore actually felt the impact of each purchase, the convenience of new tech removes some of that pain.

And even before we've reached the checkout, shops are already tempting us to spend more. Retailers – both online and physical – use a range of pricing strategies to influence how much we're willing to spend, and to coax those hard-earned pounds out of our wallet – or our debit card, mobile or even wearable tech such as watches, as the case may be.

These challenges are just some of the many factors that come in to play while we try to cover the basics and make ends meet.

OSTRICH EFFECT

Despite the widespread popularity of the myth, the ostrich does not actually bury its head in the sand in an attempt to avoid the harsh realities of the savannah. The reason these avian giants peek their heads underground is to turn the eggs that they have laid in a hole for protection. Nevertheless, it is so tempting to believe the myth that the ostrich is dim-witted (bird-brained?) enough to think that if it can't see its predators, then the predators can't see it, because that sentiment strikes close to the heart.

Consider this: have you ever been surprised when your card was declined? Avoided opening bills or emails from your bank? Or maybe you haven't had any serious adverse financial events such as being overdrawn or defaulting on a loan, but you would be hard-pressed to know how much money is in your account, what your credit card balance is or what your accumulated wealth is. You wouldn't be alone. An ING international survey found that 1 in 10 people who have personal debt don't know how much they owe, and this figure did not include mortgage debt.

This psychological phenomenon, known by behavioural scientists as 'the ostrich effect', is our way of 'protecting' ourselves from potentially distressing information. Even those who have plenty to play with are susceptible to this: people check their investment portfolio more frequently when its value is going up than when it is falling. No one likes bad news.

The problem is that this selective attention is false protection: just because we don't open our credit card bill doesn't mean that the balance owed miraculously disappears. Just as the ostrich's predators can still see her even when she can't see them, our creditors still know we owe them even if we choose to ignore it. Additionally, on a more basic level, a head in the sand means an absence of information. As obvious as it sounds, without information you can't evaluate your baseline situation, so it is impossible to tell whether you are heading in the right direction, temporarily veering off course or falling deeper still into financial distress.

Simply put – if you don't know where you are, it is hard to know how to change course. Being better informed about your financial position can improve your sense of control, which is an important aspect for financial wellbeing.

FACING UP

It may be painful now, but your future self will thank you for paying attention to how you are spending, saving, borrowing and investing today. While wanting to steer clear of distressing information may be a natural feeling, there are some approaches we can take to overcome it.

One approach is to make the required information practically unavoidable. Instead of relying on yourself to look for the information, let the information come to you. See what your bank offers, since many apps allow you to receive automatic updates with account balances or transaction notifications.

Another approach is to make it a habit. When something becomes habitual, the deliberation is stripped out of it, almost as if you are on auto-pilot. So if you recognize your own susceptibility to the ostrich effect, consider trying to make it a habit to face up to your finances. To do this, think about both the trigger to start your routine and the reward for achieving it.

Set a cue to remind yourself to assess your finances. This trigger can be as low tech or high tech as you like. An alarm or reminder on your phone is easy, but even a Post-It Note on your calendar may suffice. The point is to set aside a regular time to routinely review where you are.

Your routine will depend on your own financial position and personal situation. This could be anything from checking that you haven't gone overdrawn, to reassessing your asset allocation in your retirement portfolio.

Finally, pick a reward to bundle with this chore. According to Katherine Milkman and colleagues, knowing that a reward will be unlocked only once you've carried out your tasks at hand will help to keep you motivated. It is important that the indulgence you choose doesn't counterbalance the gains you are making by reviewing your finances. In other words, it shouldn't cost too much! For example, hold off on enjoying the next episode of that must-watch series until after you've completed your routine.

It is important to look at both our overall financial position and our main account balance or buffer. Peter Ruberton and colleagues found that people's current account balances are a particularly important component of how they feel about their finances. The researchers found that people tend to have a higher perceived sense of wellbeing (in this case, more confident and less likely to lose sleep

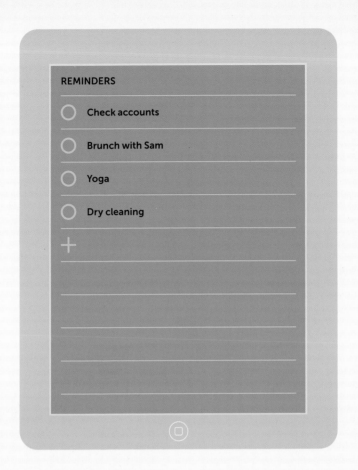

over money worries) if their readily available money is higher. A current account balance is a very salient datum: it is easy to access, understand and compare to yesterday's or last week's balance. But for many people, their account balance is only one of many financial products, including student loans, savings accounts, pensions, mortgages, car loans, investments or cash under the mattress. Liquid (easily accessible) wealth is certainly important for financial and general wellbeing, but don't forget the other components of your finances.

As we have seen, in many cases it is better to pay more attention to our finances. In the case of investors, however, it could be worthwhile to devote *less* attention. Checking their position too often (like a hypervigilant meerkat) may create the temptation to sell at a downturn in an attempt to stem losses. If your plan is to take the long view while investing, it could be worth checking less frequently, focusing on trends rather than blips.

Having the bigger picture on your financial position is an important part of taking control.

FROM CASH TO CASHLESS

Think back to the last thing you bought; how did you pay for it? Did you use cash, card, bank transfer, gift voucher or maybe some other method? Now open up your wallet: how much cash is inside?

The answer to these questions will depend on a number of factors, not least your own habits, the payment infrastructure available to you and the social norms where you live. Take Sweden, for example: the total value of cash transactions is just 2% of the value of all transactions, meaning that when Swedes do use cash, it is mostly for very small purchases. Similarly, an international survey of nearly 13,000 Europeans finds that cash is often used to buy coffee and snacks, while non-cash methods cover larger expenses such as housing costs or utilities.

As more and more financial transactions across the world are being carried out without cash, it is worth reflecting on the relative benefits and drawbacks of cash versus non-cash methods of payment. In the 'pro' column for cash, it is relatively private and widely accepted. In the 'con' column, you have to access it from somewhere – a cash machine or bank – carry it with you, and if it is stolen there's not much chance of getting it back. Non-cash payments, on the other hand, are convenient and arguably more secure, but lack privacy.

Another difference is particularly quirky. When we pay with non-cash methods, we lose the visual and tactile feedback that we get from paying with cash – feedback that changes the 'pain of paying' and our subsequent spending behaviour.

That's right – it is actually painful to encounter expensive goods, according to professor Brian Knutson and colleagues, who found that seeing high prices activates the same area of the brain as when people experience disgust or pain. The 'pain of paying' differs when making cash or non-cash transactions. The reason for this, as explained by behavioural economist Dan Ariely, is the salience of the payment. More specifically, both the timing and medium affect how we feel about parting with our money. To many of us, cash feels more like real money than a plastic card, and therefore is more painful to spend.

Cash impacts us in other ways, too. For example, whether a note is crisp and clean versus torn and tatty influences our likelihood to spend it, because we tend to hang on to the former and rid our wallet of the latter. And even the denomination, the value of the note, affects how we spend – which wouldn't happen when going cashless because there is no denomination to 'break'.

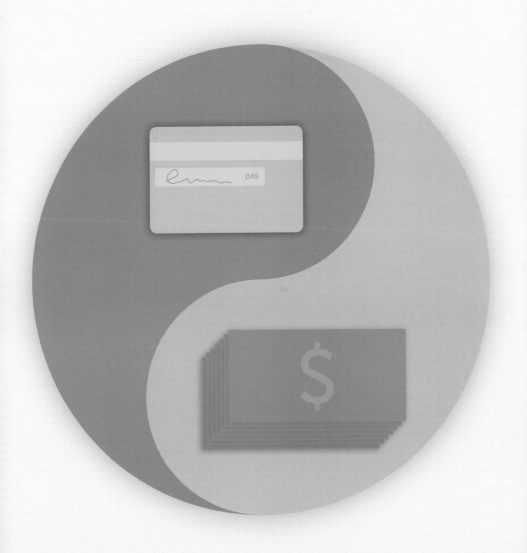

PAIN OF PAYING

The decision around how to use money isn't likely to be a blanket choice of whether to stick to only cash or to go completely cashless. There are a number of different factors that come into play, including the continuously developing digital payments infrastructure and evolving social norms. It is likely that many people will continue to use many different types of payment mechanisms.

However, as an informed consumer, it is worth keeping the differences between cash and non-cash transactions in mind, finding the method of payment with the right balance of convenience and feedback for your own personal situation.

For example, in the case of credit cards, they decouple the payment from the purchase. We buy things in a store today and pay for them only when the bill arrives up to a month later (if indeed we pay off the balance in full). This delay eliminates the instant feedback we'd get at the time of consumption if using cash, reducing the salience of the payment. In other words, it feels less painful to pay with a credit card both because it is not cash and the money doesn't actually leave our account until well after the memory of the purchase has faded.

Some new products are attempting to reintroduce the visual and tactile feedback that we miss out on when using non-cash methods. The RSA, a think-tank in London, has a long-running annual design challenge, where people are invited to submit their design in response to various societal challenges. One of the winning entries for the 2017 'Mind Your Money' brief was successful because it put visual feedback into the cashless payment equation. University student Liam Tuckwood designed a feature

that could be built in to debit or credit cards. The idea is simple and effective. A line drawing of a face, about the size of a thumbprint, sits in the corner of the card. When your balance is healthy, the face smiles; when not, the face frowns. What makes this especially clever is that of all the visual cues that could be used, the human face – even if stylized – is so easily recognizable. In fact, we are so sensitive to this that people tend to 'see' human faces in a whole host of places that are decidedly not human.

Banks and fin techs are continuously developing new products and services, and honing their apps to provide new features for their customers. They can use the pain of paying to our benefit. Some have built features such as transaction notifications with haptic feedback, helping us remain mindful of our spending behaviour without sacrificing the convenience of cashless payment.

To reduce the 'pain of paying', which may be useful for people who find it really unpleasant to spend (the 'tightwads' of Lesson 1), try pre-paying for a purchase so that the payment is decoupled from the consumption, and use a debit card or transfers over cash. To increase the pain of paying, which may be useful for 'spendthrifts', to help curb spending, try the opposite. For example, this could be by using cash at point of consumption, but this has obvious inconveniences, as discussed earlier.

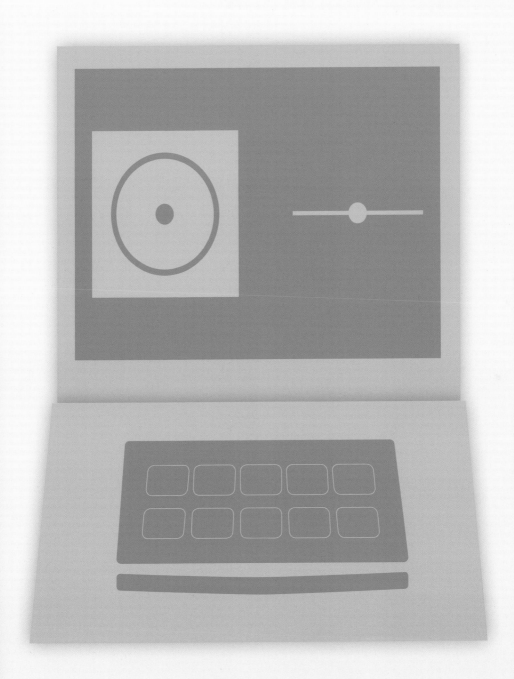

FRICTION C
CURB IMPU
SPENDING.

AN HELP
LSIVE

FRICTION

Just yesterday I hailed a taxi from my phone when my normal public transportation was suspended. It had been a long day and was getting late so, while in the car, I placed an order for a meal to be delivered. The driver dropped me off a little early, near the corner shop because I needed to pick up some milk for tomorrow morning's breakfast, which I paid for by waving my phone past the card reader. Milk safely in the fridge, I transferred some money to my sister for the gift we are getting our mum, flopped down on the sofa and ordered the next episode of my favourite turn-off-the-brain sitcom.

In that short time I never even opened my wallet. The apps we have at our disposal make it seamless and easy to pay for our daily goings on. This ease of use is seen by many – consumers, tech designers and banks alike – as being unquestionably good. After all, better for something to be easy than for it to be hard, right? As payment methods and business models develop, the friction is designed out of the process, so much so that we've now come to expect speed and simplicity from our quotidian purchases.

But is it possible that it has become too easy, leading us down the path of unwanted spending? Take subscriptions: when companies make it easy to subscribe to a service but difficult to leave, people can end up making monthly payments for something they don't use (gym membership, anyone?).

Yes, adding friction can drive people away by making the activity too difficult, but slowing people down can also be beneficial, warding off errors and preventing them from inadvertently carrying out an action that otherwise might be too easy to do. More importantly, slowness can help curb impulsive spending. This is useful for any spendthrift and potentially especially valuable for people experiencing mental health issues, who may be spending manically to feel better. Whether it is to manage impulsivity, a shopping addiction or other vulnerabilities, optional restrictions or alerts that people can set up while in a 'cold state' to kick in during a 'hot state' (in certain stores, or during periods of manic spending) could be helpful to prevent racking up bills for spending that feels good in the moment but may be regretted later.

Chequebooks seem antiquated these days, and they also represent the ultimate in friction. While not advocating for a return to chequebooks, it's worth noting that using cheques may improve your overview of finances, because the act of writing the amount in numbers and words has been found to help people remember their spending more accurately than when using a credit card. The more accurately we recall previous purchases, the better we can plan our future ones.

Rent $ ~~~~

Water bill $ ~~~

Dinner with Juan $ ~~~

Gift for mum $ ~~~

MINDLESS TO MINDFUL

While low-friction transactions are sought out by many, there is arguably a case for making them a little less slick and a little more *rough*. Of course everyone likes convenience, but when you are offered a product that seems really easy, consider whether this is the best option for you.

A purposefully low tech submission to the RSA Student Design Awards was one of my favourites: a piece of plastic that you could snap onto your debit card, the same size as the card itself. On the plastic was a set of four sliders and a question in each, such as: *Is this under £100? Did I sleep well last night?* The card cover would come with some preset questions, but a person could always print his or her own questions suited to their particular needs. The idea is that you have to move the sliders to the *yes* or *no* position and need 4 out of 4 to be at yes before the card is released and can be inserted into a cashpoint or card reader.

Sound a bit extreme? Well, even if the whole card-being-locked-in-plastic part were to be dropped, just the act of being confronted with these questions each time you wish to pay may help to slow down the process, turning it from easy and automatic to a more thoughtful transaction. In other words, it could help the activity to move from being mindless to mindful. For payments through mobile or digital devices you could have a digital version of the sliders, the task of answering the questions spurring the spender to reflect on the impending purchase.

Being faced with questions each time we wish to pay may help move spending from being mindless to mindful.

Apps can also increase friction, for example by making a user interact with different parts of the screen by making certain features less obvious or by making the action a swipe instead of a tap because it is easier to unintentionally tap than unintentionally swipe. Look out for how apps and websites are designed – are the sellers making it too easy to spend money with them?

If a low-friction option is still preferred, consider that as friction decreases it is even more important to keep track of spending. So find out what your bank can offer you in terms of balance and transaction notifications and refer back to Lesson 5 for tips on how to avoid being an ostrich.

THAT'S A BARGAIN! (OR IS IT?)

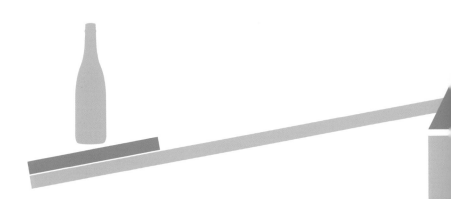

It's hard to know how much it costs to make most of the things we buy, whether it's a beer, a bowling ball or a bathroom suite. What are these things made of, and how much do those raw materials cost? What about the labour, shipping, distribution and marketing?

As we are usually unable to calculate the costs that went into producing something to identify what a minimum or fair price for it would be, perhaps the price should reflect the value it brings. But that, too, is a hard question. We find it difficult to judge the absolute value of something, and instead think in terms of relative value compared to other products or reference points. Being unsure of the 'real' value of something means that what we're willing to pay is often open to suggestion, and retailers can price their goods to take advantage. **Anchoring** and **decoys** are two approaches to look out for.

Companies can use price to signal quality. Beer brand Stella Artois used to quip in their long-standing ad campaign that their beverage is 'reassuringly expensive'. And surprisingly, with a higher price, we may not only expect that the product will be of better quality but also actually experience it as better. A study by Baba Shiv, Ziv Carmon and Dan Ariely found that price matters. People who paid about half as much for an energy drink claiming to help with 'mental acuity' then went on to solve fewer word puzzles than people who had paid full price, despite the drink being exactly the same for both groups.

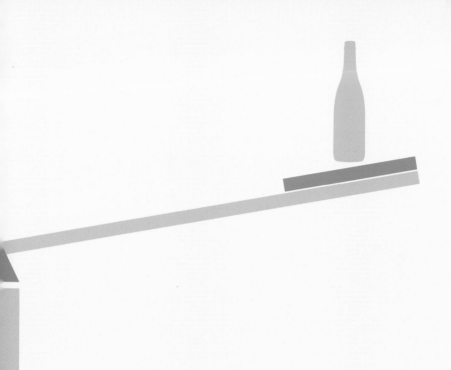

ANCHORING

The first number we consider in a purchasing decision can serve as an 'anchor' for how much we are willing to pay for an item, even when the anchor is completely arbitrary. In one study, people were shown a range of items, from wine to computer accessories. In the first part of the task, they were asked to list the last two digits of their social security number, and then to put a dollar sign in front of it. Then for each item they were asked two questions: whether they would pay more or less than this completely arbitrary and randomly assigned amount, and how much they would be willing to pay for it. Even though the number shouldn't have had any bearing on their valuation, the researchers found that it did. Incredibly, people with the highest social security numbers were, on average, willing to pay more for the products than those with the lowest numbers.

DECOY EFFECT

When it is hard to compare two products, maybe because they have many different attributes (e.g. digital cameras) or are just very different from each other (a magazine subscription in print versus digital), introducing a product that is similar, but slightly worse, than one of the options can shift our preferences. The inferior 'decoy' product highlights the relative strength of the option it is inferior to. Dan Ariely explains that you might not have a strong view whether an online magazine subscription for $59 is better or worse value than a subscription for print plus online for $125, but when a third option of print only for $125 (which is clearly worse value than print plus online) is introduced, many will choose the combo. Retailers can also use last year's model, at the same or higher price, as a decoy to help shift sales of a given product.

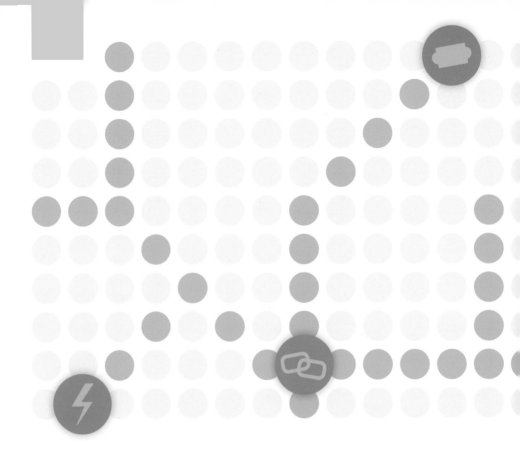

TRUE VALUE

We are faced with innumerable purchasing decisions as we go about our daily lives. Navigating them can be tricky, not just because of the sheer volume, but also because it is actually quite difficult to know what anything is really worth. Understanding that retailers can use this to their advantage is the first step in trying to avoid getting reeled in by clever pricing techniques.

When comparing products, it may be helpful to think of the opportunity costs of the difference in price. That is, what else could you buy with the money you save by buying the cheaper version, or what would you need to give up if you buy the more expensive one?

If I buy the good-enough jacket over the premium one, I can also get a pair of gloves, go out for a nice meal or top up my savings buffer. These trade-off calculations can be tiresome to work through, but may help to put an item's value into perspective.

Check whether you've been influenced by a high anchor, for example by an initial price slashed down to a sale price. Use anchoring to your advantage when negotiating – whether for a lower price in a bazaar or for a higher starting salary at your next job. Using a very low (or high) number as a starting consideration may influence how far the other party is willing to compromise.

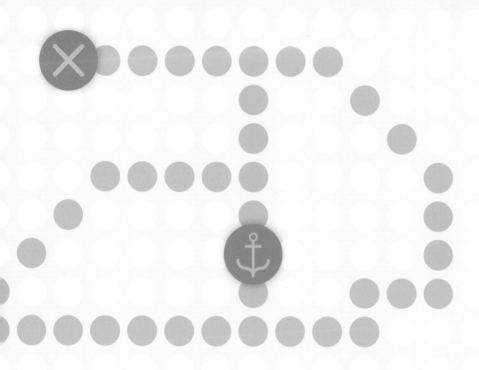

What other products are shown nearby (whether in store or online) that are irrelevant to your choice, either because they are inferior or because they are ridiculously expensive? If you can identify decoys it may help your effort to ignore them. While window shopping for luxury goods may seem a bit of fun, it is worth considering whether those new reference points could influence your other shopping.

Of course, there are many other ways in which retailers might encourage us to pay more. Bundling their products can make it difficult to determine the individual price of each component of the bundle, and therefore more difficult to compare to alternative brands or products. When faced with a bundle, spend an extra minute to calculate if the bundled price is really better than the sum of its parts. Do you actually want everything included in the bundle?

Companies might price their goods and services based on what it costs to provide them, what is generally considered fair or the value they believe it brings to customers. But since perceived value is subjective and open to suggestion, they can use techniques such as anchoring, bundling or using a decoy product, to increase our willingness to pay for our wants and needs.

TOOLKIT

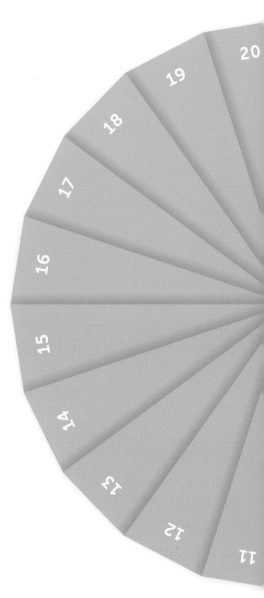

05

Head in the sand? It can be tempting to avoid learning what could potentially be bad news. But not facing up to where your finances stand makes it hard to see where changes could be made, and impossible to know whether those changes are making a meaningful impact. Make it easier for yourself to pay attention to your finances by bundling the chore with some small reward.

06

Cash, debit cards, bank transfers, gift vouchers – they're all the same, right? Wrong. When we pay with non-cash methods, we lose important feedback that we would get if paying with cash; cash can be more 'painful' to part with. So as technology moves us towards cashlessness, it may be easier to spend more than budgeted. Find the method of payment that has the appropriate balance of convenience and feedback for you.

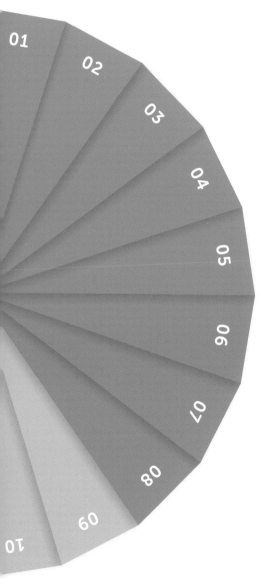

07

As payment methods and business models develop for convenience, speed and simplicity, friction is designed out of the process. This ease of use is seen by many as being unquestionably good. But is it possible that it has become too easy, leading us down the path of unwanted spending? Think about the apps you use and whether a little more friction in the process would be worthwhile. When spending is easy, keeping track of incomings and outgoings becomes even more important to stay in control.

08

We are faced with innumerable purchasing decisions as we go about our lives. But it is hard to know the true value of anything. We think of the value of products not in absolute terms but rather in relation to other products. Using price to signal quality, anchoring us onto high prices or introducing decoy products are among the many techniques sellers can use to encourage us to spend more.

FURTHER LEARNING

READ

Predictably Irrational: The hidden forces that shape our decisions
Dan Ariely (Harper, 2010)

IIS Cashless Society Survey
ING (2017) eZonomics.com

LISTEN

We shouldn't stick our heads in the sand, but we do it anyway
Hidden Brain podcast
npr.org

Why are we still using cash?
Freakonomics podcast
freakonomics.com/podcast

WATCH

The Decoy Effect
National Geographic explains how our decision-making changes when a decoy is thrown into the mix.
video.nationalgeographic.com/tv/brain-games/the-decoy-effect

The Pain of Paying
Dan Ariely explains the concept in this YouTube video.

DO

Experiment on yourself
Try one week using cash only, and another week using no cash at all. How did you feel? How did your spending change?

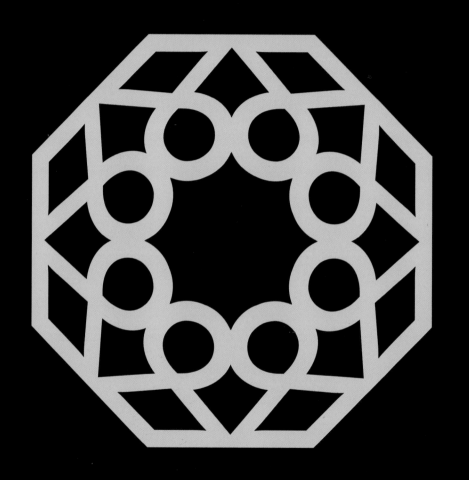

RESILIENCE

LESSONS

Having a buffer to cover emergencies is crucial. An unexpected expense can tip someone from being in the 'chugging along just fine' zone into a murky pool of stress and unmanageable debt.

No one has a crystal ball. So we can't ever be sure what we'll be faced with tomorrow. That's why a key component of financial wellbeing is building in resilience to shocks – whether that shock is an unforeseen expense, such as a car repair, or a change to income, like a pay cut or bout of unemployment.

Having a buffer to cover emergencies is crucial. An unexpected expense can tip someone from being in the 'chugging along just fine' zone into a murky pool of stress and unmanageable debt. As discussed earlier, while wealth begets wealth, financial insecurity can beget insecurity.

For example, without a buffer it might be tempting to use a payday lender or other form of short-term credit such as credit cards or overdrafts, which become an even more expensive choice as interest accumulates and late fees are incurred. Many turn to these short-term debts for rainy days, and there are a number of ways that we don't pay them back in textbook fashion.

When money is really tight, juggling it is cognitively demanding; it can lead us to focus so exclusively on our immediate financial issues, leaving little headspace with which to contemplate other opportunities in our lives. If you are invited to a last-minute interview for the job of your dreams, something as routine as finding a babysitter brings a whole set of new negotiations if there is no slack in the budget to pay her.

While hard work and talent are important, sometimes life is down to luck, so having a buffer to fall back on is important. People tend to be pretty optimistic, thinking that bad things won't happen to them personally, and overconfident that if bad things *were* to happen, they could find a way to overcome them. These frames of mind, while they have their benefits, can leave us unprepared if we do experience bad luck.

Unexpected emergency expenses or dips in income can be the trigger that starts a financially unhealthy spiral. When struggling to keep up, being in this scarcity mindset can perpetuate the problem, which highlights why it is so important to move the dial from optimism to realism and plan accordingly to keep ourselves financially resilient to these surprises.

ROLE OF LUCK IN SUCCESS

Although you're unlikely to be a lucky lottery winner, you've almost certainly experienced some luck in your life. Luck, in the sense it is used here, is not just good fortune; it could also be bad luck, misfortune. Both are completely outside of your control.

Luck plays a larger role in success than many tend to appreciate. This finding, explored in depth by Cornell professor Robert Frank, might be because people tend to remember instances of bad luck more so than instances of good luck, or possibly because those who are successful find it easier to believe that they got there through their own actions (because it protects their egos) than to attribute it to outside events. Generally, we prefer to believe that the world is just and fair, in an attempt to help make sense of life. This lack of awareness of our headwinds or tailwinds has interesting financial implications.

Of course this does not mean that financial success is *purely* down to luck. Frank's point is that hard work and talent are necessary too, but are often not sufficient conditions for success. Successful people's decisions and actions on a day-to-day basis, and the way they cultivate their own passions, undoubtedly create a large part of their success, however, other people work hard and nurture their talent, too. But

near the top the margins are close, and luck can make the difference between first and second place. In our competitive, globalized world, the difference in rewards between second and first place is often substantial, therefore the marginal gains from being lucky are perhaps felt more than they were previously.

Several centuries ago, to be a market winner you had to be the best in your town, village or within your trading network. Now, the area within which you must be 'the best' has grown enormously. Take, for example, selling a bedframe: previously, the effort of shipping something so heavy would make it likely that most people would buy from their local furniture maker; now companies sell globally, and almost instantly. For this reason, the implications of being in first place versus second place – and therefore the consequences of good or bad luck – are heightened.

An important distinction should also be noted between luck and privilege. Some people were lucky to be born into privilege: they grew up with more resources, more stable environments or access to better schools than others. This certainly provides them with an advantage in life, and further bad or good luck may balance or amplify this advantage over the course of their lives.

If forces outside of our control do play such a large role, one could argue that there is no point in planning for the future. Who knows what will happen tomorrow? But another way to look at this is that precisely because luck – good or bad – affects our lives, it is important to both plan for negative eventualities and take more traditional positive actions to work towards success, such as putting in the effort and developing our skills.

READY TO RECEIVE LUCK

By definition, it is impossible to control luck. But you can put yourself in situations where if you *were* to be lucky you would be in a good position to make the best use of that luck. Just as a seed is no good without soil, a stroke of good luck is most impactful if our life 'field' is tilled and ready to receive it. Equipping oneself with the right tools to make use of good fortune is likely achieved through hard work, up-skilling yourself and being in the right place at the right time.

Thinking about what our strengths and weaknesses are might be a first step. Already good at something? Build on this to become even better, so that you acquire a specialization. Really terrible at something else? Think about how you can make yourself a little bit less terrible at it. This doesn't have to be daunting. Mastering a small, repeatable task within a larger field may be a small win, which then boosts motivation to attempt to master other related tasks. That way, even if good luck takes time to reach you, you'll be building up your skills base in the meanwhile.

We should be aware of our success and proud of the work we've done to get there, but also try to humbly appreciate the role of factors outside our control that have helped us along the way. The following simple exercise studied by researcher Yuezhou Huo might help: pick something about your life that you personally would categorize as a success. Write it down. Now reflect on this success and try to identify three specific events or forces outside of your control that helped you achieve that success.

There are a number of potential collateral benefits to this thought experiment: generosity, wellbeing and possibly even improved opportunity. Research found that people who listed the factors outside of their control were more generous towards others than people who listed factors within their control. Specifically, they donated more of their earnings from their participation in the research to charity. Consider, too, that by reflecting on the conditions surrounding your previous luck, it might help you to anticipate where you have the best chances of 'being discovered' by luck in the future.

Robert Frank argues for a progressive consumption tax to counteract the ill-effects of misfortune on some members of society. He argues for people to be taxed not on what they earn, but on what they spend on discretionary items, in other words, the goods and services that are above the basics. The tax would get higher the more you spend, so that basic rent would not be taxed but the new yacht would be. This type of taxation would curb luxury spending while not hurting lower spenders, and the tax earned by the government could be used to fund infrastructure that supports everyone, rich or poor, such as better roads and schools.

Just as a seed is no good without soil, a stroke of good luck is most impactful if our life 'field' is tilled and ready to receive it.

ROSE-TINTED GLASSES

When you think of your future, what do you expect? Overall, will things have gone well – is your future self earning more and the economy booming? Or not so well – have you or a loved one become sick or lost a job?

If you are like most people, the future looks pretty bright; our optimism keeps us believing that good things will come. Optimism is important for a number of reasons, but, unfortunately, just because we believe and expect our future to be rosy, does not guarantee that it actually will be. And this is where our bias towards being optimistic can be problematic.

Researchers use a range of methods to measure the level of optimism bias. For example, some studies ask people's expectations about future events and then measure whether and how those events actually transpired. This could be anything from the starting salary on our next job, how much we'll enjoy a future holiday or the number of positive events that will happen in the next month. When our expectations are systematically higher than the reality, this is an optimism bias.

Another study used the extent to which people overestimate their life expectancy as a measure of optimism. Survey respondents were asked 'About how long do you think you will live?' Researchers Manju Puri and

David Robinson then contrasted people's self-reported life expectancy with the age they are statistically likely to live to, given their various lifestyle factors. Those who believe they will live longer than the actuarial tables predict were considered optimistic.

This study further differentiated between moderate and extreme optimists with some intriguing findings. Moderate optimism is

hours and expect their overall career to be longer.

The problem for financial wellbeing is therefore not moderate optimism but extreme optimism. Being overly optimistic can leave us unprepared for life's downturns. Puri and Robinson found that extreme optimists worked fewer hours, saved less money, and held a higher proportion of their wealth in illiquid (not easily accessible) assets. Presumably extreme optimists underestimate the likelihood of negative events happening to them and expect that everything will turn out fine, so there's no need to build a buffer or have quick access to cash.

Researchers recently found that people typically expect that both their income and expenses will increase in the future, but underestimate the extent to which the expenses will increase, a phenomenon Jonathan Berman and colleagues termed *expense neglect*. Similarly, other research found that people tend to overspend on infrequent 'exceptional' expenses. The idea here is that because it is thought of as exceptional, we think about them on a case-by-case basis, so it doesn't seem too bad to slightly overextend 'just this once' – but of course they all add up. This combination of underestimating and overspending could leave us feeling the pinch in the future.

correlated with a range of positive outcomes, from better health and being more likely to remarry after a divorce, to better financial behaviour, like paying your credit card bill on time and saving more. Optimism lays a solid foundation for us to exert willpower (see Lesson 19), as it helps us believe that our efforts now will pay off in the future. Indeed, moderate optimists work longer

PLAN FOR THE WORST, HOPE FOR THE BEST

How can we correct our optimism bias? Would simply learning the actual probabilities for a range of events help? Sounds reasonable. However, neuroscientist Tali Sharot tested this approach and found that we are surprisingly resistant to updating our beliefs. More precisely, we update selectively: when we learn information that is better than we predicted, we update our outlook, but when that information is worse than we had predicted (and therefore should correct our optimism), we don't update our beliefs very much at all. It seems that we learn only what we want to hear.

While extreme optimism is financially imprudent, extreme pessimism doesn't seem desirable either. It is possible that one could scrimp and save for decades, missing out on soul-enriching experiences, just to be struck by some tragic accident. On the other hand, it is also entirely possible that one could live a life of hedonism and instant gratification, squandering money and failing to invest in skills for the future, then go on to live a long life, and in old age be unable to work and have no savings to fall back on. Pictures of financial futures are often painted in extremes like these, while the reality will likely be somewhere in the middle.

Life is full of both risk and uncertainty. Events happen and opportunities arise that we cannot foresee. So when we are doing our financial planning, we each need to find the balance that feels most appropriate for ourselves.

Given the range of benefits moderate optimism provides, it seems a good idea to keep a relatively rosy outlook, while also being prepared for nasty surprises that may come our way.

One technique, advocated by Nobel-prize-winning psychologist Daniel Kahneman, is the pre-mortem. This thought experiment has you imagining that your project, finances or life has turned out to be a horrible disaster. What happened? As you build up this picture it prompts reflection on what could be done to prevent the situation or to mitigate the consequences of it.

If this kind of scary scenario planning isn't for you, at a less existentially threatening level a simple rule of thumb could be to review next year's budget, take whatever you expect your expenses to be – and add more. This may correct the *expense neglect* we tend to have. Check that your savings buffer is adequate, and consider what insurances are appropriate for you.

Perhaps the trick is to plan for a worst-case scenario, while allowing yourself the levity to believe that it won't happen. As the saying goes: 'expect the best, plan for the worst and prepare to be surprised'.

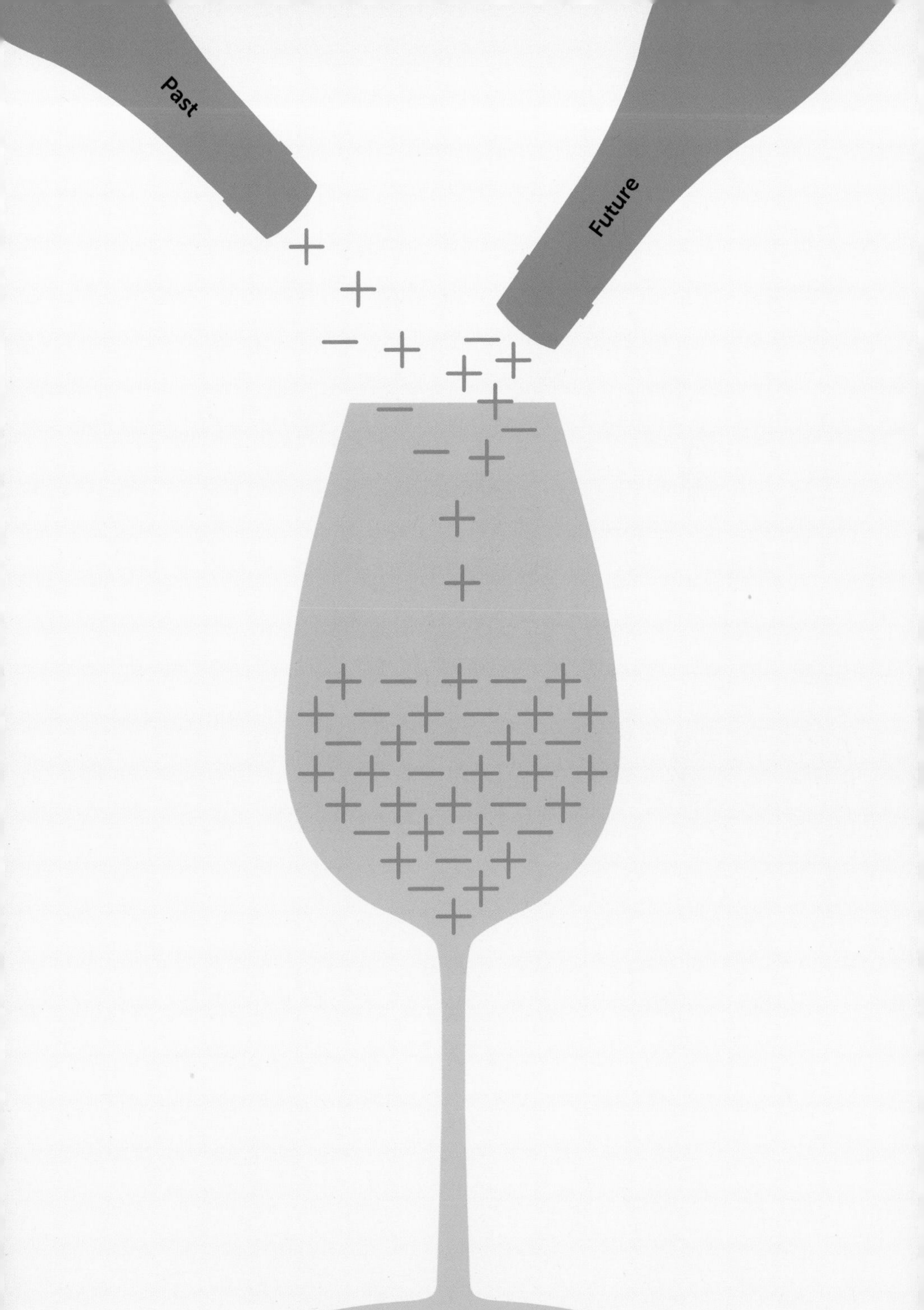
Past
Future

SUPRISES
ARE YOU F
PREPEARED

HAPPEN.
NANCIALLY
FOR THEM?

THE ATTENTION TAX

Years ago there was an ad on TV showing people on a basketball court, with a simple question: how many times is the basketball passed? I carefully counted each pass of the ball, feeling pretty confident about my answer. But instead of announcing the correct figure, the ad asked 'Did you see the woman in the petticoat?' A person dressed head to toe in a ridiculous costume had walked straight through the basketball game. And I had absolutely not noticed it.

Because our attention is limited, when we need to devote headspace to managing our finances, it can be difficult to retain enough attention for other important decisions in our lives.

A useful way to think about this constraint is by comparing the size of your budget and the amount of expenses you have to the size of a suitcase and the amount of stuff you need to pack into it. When there is plenty of room because you have a very big suitcase (a lot of money), it is fairly easy to fit everything in that you need (cover your expenses). But when the suitcase is small or your requirements are large, this task is more difficult and the decision-making process becomes more complex. Whether you bring your flip flops now depends not just on whether you think you need them, but also on what you will need to leave out to make room

for them. These trade-off decisions are cognitively demanding. They require a lot of headspace – or, as behavioural scientists Sendhil Mullainathan and Eldar Shafir call it, cognitive bandwidth.

Mullainathan, Shafir and their colleagues have conducted extensive research on this topic, from shopping malls in New Jersey to farms in rural India. They find that in periods of scarcity, when people don't have much money, they tend to tunnel their attention nearly exclusively on the immediate task at hand. While this can have advantages, it can also exacerbate the problem, creating a vicious cycle. Because in times of financial scarcity people use up cognitive bandwidth making difficult trade-offs, there is less headspace left over for making other important decisions.

For example, they find that the farmers score lower on tests that measure fluid intelligence (problem-solving and reasoning skills) immediately before the sugar cane harvest, when money is scarce, than immediately after the harvest, in a time of plenty. The difference in test scores was equivalent to roughly 13 IQ points, or a night's sleep, showing that experiencing financial hardship imposes a 'mental tax' on us. This means that it can be hardest to pull ourselves out of financial difficulty in the very times that we need the most help.

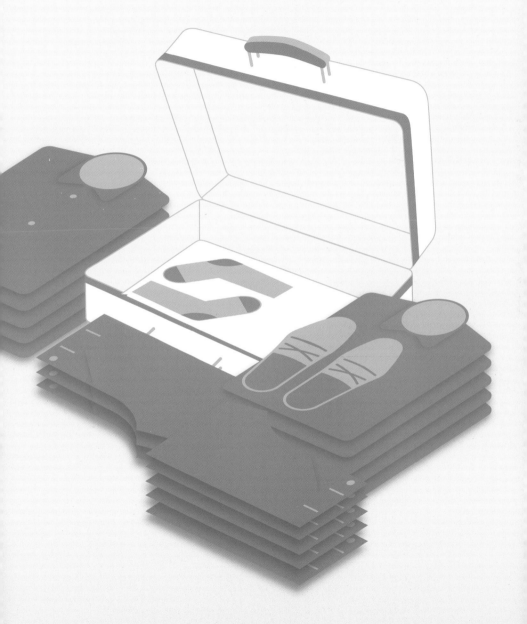

CREATING HEADSPACE

US President Barack Obama reportedly wore just one of two different suits throughout his term of office because he didn't want to use up precious headspace deciding what to wear when there were more important decisions to be made. So what can we do to simplify our lives when we find ourselves without the required headspace to make good decisions?

Getting help with hard decisions or finding ways to replenish our attention may help. For example, try to get a second opinion on a decision from someone trusted. If you have the possibility to sleep on it, do so. If you have the luxury of rescheduling the decision to a time when you will be less constrained and/or overrun with other decisions, take advantage of that. We live in an age in which people expect answers more quickly than ever, but it is amazing what a holding email can do.

Mullainathan and Shafir suggest that organizations can make life easier for people in a number of ways. For example, they can design their products or processes so that the default option is one that would be helpful for many people. Behavioural science research has shown we tend to follow the status quo, and incredibly,

this can hold even if we are told that the default is randomly determined. Given the power of defaults on people's behaviour, it is especially important that the default in these cases minimizes an adverse impact on people rather than maximizing the benefit of some.

Additionally, companies can provide supporting (and free) services that will relieve people of competing demands on their attention – by providing a crèche service, for example.

Of course, changing organizations is difficult. We can use our voting power to support appropriate policies, and our professional power to advocate changes in the workplace and suggest process improvements for customers and staff. The key is to empathize with the people using your products and services to create an environment that best serves people's limited cognitive bandwidth.

The self-reinforcing nature of this problem makes it a tricky one to tackle, but it does highlight the benefit of building up some easily accessible buffer savings for those occasions when your expenses are edging towards exceeding your available balance.

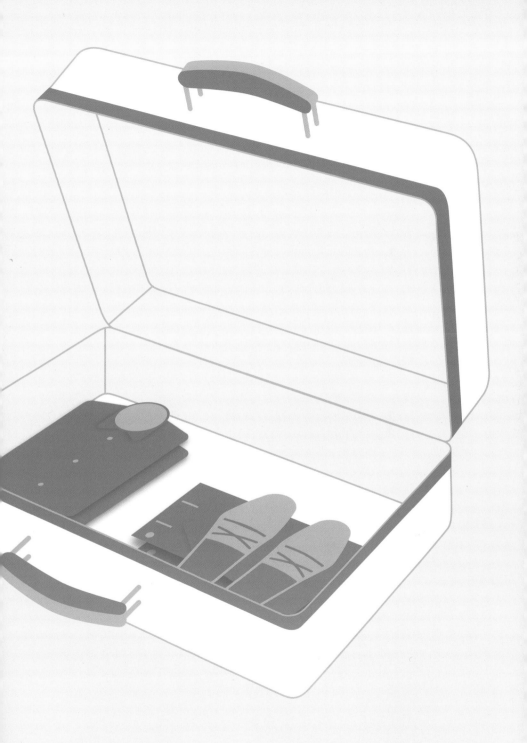

DEALING WITH DEBT

Credit cards, personal loans, overdrafts, even a favour from a friend. Debts can add up. With potentially many different debts to juggle, how should someone go about paying them off? Which debts should get priority?

Mathematically, the answer is clear: make all minimum repayments and then pay down the debt with the highest interest charges.

However, humans don't always behave in textbook fashion, and this is certainly true of debt repayment. Sometimes, even if we have the money available (say in a savings account), we won't use it to pay down debt, even though the interest charges make it expensive for us to hang on to any of that debt. Other times, instead of paying down the most expensive debt, we pay down the smallest, or we pay down a share of each debt. And when it comes to our credit cards, having the minimum repayment amount shown prominently can actually influence us to repay less of the balance than we otherwise might. Let's look at each of these in turn.

Co-holding

Holding both savings and debt can be costly, because the interest earned on savings is almost always lower than the interest charged on debt. In other words, debt costs you more and will grow faster than what you earn on your savings. Economists call having both debt and sufficient liquid assets co-holding, and despite the expense, studies in the USA and UK have found that many people do just this. Behavioural economists John Gathergood and Joerg Weber found that roughly 12% of households surveyed in the UK co-hold, leading to approximately £650 in extra interest charges per year. Note that this extra cost is totally unnecessary, because had they used their money to pay down their debt, they would have avoided incurring it.

Paying down debt

When we do pay our debt down, rather than paying off the most expensive debt first, sometimes people use a range of other approaches. For example, researchers find that some people pay off the smallest-valued debts first, regardless of interest rate, apparently in an effort to reduce the number of open debts. This approach, sometimes called snowballing, means that while people with multiple debts may be streamlining the number of accounts, they aren't paying down their total debt as quickly as possible and may incur unnecessary interest charges through that inefficiency.

Other approaches include paying down the debt with the lowest credit limit in order to mitigate the risk of exceeding it, or the one with the highest credit limit to 'create space' for a big future purchase; another is to pay an equal share to all debts. Still another is to use the balanced matching approach, which is to pay off credit card debts in the same proportion as their balances.

Hooked to the minimum

Think of your typical credit card statement. Often both the total balance and the minimum repayment stand out as being important information, so they grab our attention. Behavioural scientist Neil Stewart found that some people get anchored (see Lesson 4), or mentally hooked, on the minimum repayment amount. This is a relatively low amount, influencing us to repay less than we could afford – and therefore causing higher interest charges overall.

Different debt repayment strategies have different benefits. Some have financial gains, others might have motivational gains.

EASIER OR CHEAPER?

Are there any benefits to repaying our debts in these non-textbook ways? Or are all of these approaches just 'mistakes'?

Co-holding

Co-holders are no fools; Gathergood and Weber found that the co-holders they studied were financially literate and had a high level of education. What some co-holders did report, though, was higher than average impulsivity when spending. And so, rather than a mistake, some people may be co-holding as a way of tempering their own impulsivity. Some may purposefully keep savings untouched because once the piggy bank (metaphorical or actual) is cracked open, it'd be too easy to spend it all. The high cost of borrowing may actually be beneficial in this case, as it is an especially painful deterrent against impulsive spending.

Of course, even without this behavioural aide, there may be good reasons for holding back some liquid savings as a precautionary measure. Some expenses can't be paid by credit card, so it is worth having easy access to cash for these moments.

If you are co-holding, consider what level of precautionary savings are right for you, and reflect on whether the cost is worth it to keep your impulsivity in check. If so, then maintaining a liquid asset balance in spite of having expensive debt might be appropriate. Or perhaps consider what other commitment devices you could use to help curb impulsive spending, so that you can avoid the painful mounting interest charges.

Snowballing

Why would people 'snowball' their debt repayment, paying down the smallest debt first? It is possible that people don't fully grasp the costs, underestimating the effect of compounding interest. When researcher Moty Amar and his colleagues showed study participants the interest charges in dollars (rather than just percentages) incurred over the course of the debt, they were subsequently more likely to start repaying the debts with the highest charges.

Snowballing, while financially sub-optimal, may also have psychological and cognitive benefits. Some people may find it more motivational to chunk a bigger, abstract goal (such as being debt-free) into smaller concrete goals, and so by achieving one goal (such as closing out one particular credit card) may find it easier to make progress towards the larger goal. Reducing the number of debts may bring cognitive gains by reducing the need to keep track of multiple repayment structures and due dates. Reducing complexity may free up mental bandwidth, which could then be devoted to other financially efficient tasks.

First, understand the terms

The first step should be to review the costs and repayment terms of your debt to make sure you understand them. Consider calculating what the percentages mean in true money terms to ensure you appreciate the actual cost of borrowing. Understand how much of what you are paying back is the principal (the original amount borrowed) and how much is just the cost of borrowing.

The take home message is that, if you want the maths on your side, your best bet may be to pay off the most expensive debt first. If they all have the same rate, or if you struggle with motivation to pay down your debts, snowballing could be for you.

TOOLKIT

09

Luck plays a larger role in success than we tend to appreciate, possibly because it is easier to believe that if you are successful you got there through your own actions. Create situations for yourself where if you were to be lucky, you are already in a position to make the best use of that luck.

10

Optimism has important benefits, from motivating us out of bed in the morning, to helping us exert the willpower needed to resist temptation in service of a better future outcome. But optimism can have a downside, too, when we fail to anticipate bad events – such as losing our job, being burgled or rising future expenses – leaving us unprepared. We can't predict the future, but we can choose the scenarios that we base our financial plans on. Pre-mortems, where you consider what could go wrong and how to prevent it, and having an adequate emergency buffer could help.

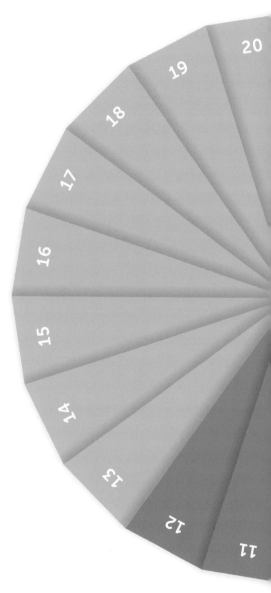

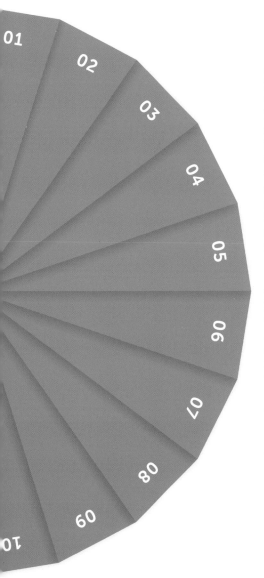

11

Not having enough money can perpetuate a situation of scarcity. On the plus side, having tight constraints can focus the mind, but on the downside, having to juggle resources is very cognitively demanding, and this demand on our headspace crowds out the ability to make decisions that are in our own self-interest. Organizations that we deal with can and should simplify their processes to help us focus on critical financial decisions.

12

Many people turn to credit cards or other short-term debt for rainy days. If holding multiple debts, the order in which you pay them down can have a big impact on the ultimate interest paid; sub-optimal repayment approaches can be expensive. It seems paradoxical to have both debt and savings (why not just use the savings to pay off the debt?) but there may be some precautionary (access to liquidity) and psychological benefits (controlling impulses) to doing so.

FURTHER LEARNING

READ

Success and Luck: Good Fortune and the Myth of Meritocracy
Robert Frank (Princeton University Press, 2016)

Scarcity: Why having too little means so much
Sendhil Mullainathan and Eldar Shafir (Allen Lane, 2013)

LISTEN

You Need an Emergency Fund
The Pineapple Project podcast
abc.net.au

WATCH

The Optimism Bias
Tali Sharot
TED Talk

Living Under Scarcity
Eldar Shafir
TED Talk

EXPLORE

Invisible Gorilla
Test your own attention
theinvisiblegorilla.com/videos.html

Years You Have Left to Live, Probably
Check out this interactive life expectancy chart for a dose of realism
flowingdata.com/2015/09/23/years-you-have-left-to-live-probably

LONG-TERM PLANNING

LESSONS

Planning for the long term is crucial and complex. It often means making trade-offs and investments for uncertain returns.

When you think about your future, what do you see? In life there are a number of big decisions to consider when planning for the long term. Housing; relationships, family, and providing for others; education and upskilling; travel and other adventures; work, professional development and retirement, to name a few. Money isn't the only consideration in these decisions, but the question of how you will finance these choices are always part of the equation.

So, how will you fund your future?

Spoiler alert: you are probably not going to win the lottery. Sorry. Neither will I. Nevertheless, it can be fun to dream, and in this section we explore why many find it tempting to partake.

Lottery winner or not, we probably *will* retire eventually, so a prudent approach would be to prepare for it. Speaking with friends, I get the sense that while none of us feel old, we know we are no longer young, and that we waited far too long to start putting money aside for retirement. And many others are in the same boat. This may be because when things seem psychologically distant, it can leave us feeling unmotivated to do much about it. So a good intention to put a retirement savings plan into place 'someday' is perpetually put off.

While there are a number of strategies we could use to help jolt ourselves into action, there are also ways in which the system could be designed better. That is, governments and employers could design structures that rely less on our good intentions and more on how our human nature actually works. Behavioural scientists call such a structure the 'choice architecture' of an experience. When the choice architecture changes, our subsequent behaviour often changes, too. More specifically, in this section we will learn what employers can do to help us put more away for our future retirement.

A curious feature of many big decisions is that they have long-term consequences, so it is hard to know straightaway whether we have made a good choice. Often, we must make some sort of immediate sacrifice or investment for benefits that only accrue sometime in the future. So when we're thinking about the trade-offs between now and the future, the extent to which we have some reliability in our lives matters. After all, immediate sacrifices are real, but future returns are merely expected, and in an unreliable environment it is even less certain that our expected returns will materialize.

These types of now versus future trade-offs are an emblematic feature of long-term planning, so gaining a richer understanding of how we tend to think about this component of financial wellbeing is key in helping us build the financial future we're hoping for.

PLAYING THE LOTTERY

In August 2017, a woman from a small town in the UK learned that she had won a six-bedroom country manor worth £845,000 by purchasing just £40 worth of lottery tickets. That same week, a woman in the USA won a $758,700,000 Powerball jackpot.

It is difficult to picture such an amount in a stack of notes, but it's a fun thought experiment to imagine the lifestyle you could have with such riches. One could argue that buying a lottery ticket is paying for the opportunity to dream. Yet the odds of winning are tiny, so why would anyone ever buy a ticket?

Research by Nobel-prize-winning psychologist Daniel Kahneman and his late collaborator Amos Tversky shows that people tend to overweight small probabilities. When chances are 100% or 0%, it is with certainty that something will or will not happen. No surprises there. But when chances are slightly below 100% or slightly above 0% we have a hard time recognizing just how close it is to certainty. Maybe, just maybe, we will be the exception to the rule and be that .000001% or similarly unlikely percentage.

Interestingly, once you buy a ticket, some other psychological phenomena kick in that make you really want to keep that particular ticket. Most people wouldn't want to sell their ticket on to someone else, even for more money. Part of this has to do with the fact that once we own something, we feel more attached to it and therefore tend to expect more money for it than we paid for it. In economics speak, our willingness to accept

exceeds our willingness to pay. If we were 'rational' – that is, if we all behaved in the way that many traditional economic theories model us to be – then it would make no sense to demand more money for something than we were willing to pay (plus any transaction costs incurred) for it. But we are not. We are human. And once something is ours we tend to subjectively value it as being worth more than when it was not ours.

Another reason we are inclined to want to hang on to our lottery tickets is as a pre-emptive measure to avoid future regret. Regret is an uncomfortable feeling, so naturally we try to avoid it, even subconsciously. Marcel Zeelenberg and Rik Pieters found that people expect to feel more regret at not playing lotteries where you

know that you would have won, for example, if your postcode doubles as your lottery numbers. In a traditional lottery setup, where you pick your numbers or get randomly allocated numbers, you won't know whether you would have won – unless, of course, you always pick the same set of numbers (your lucky combo) or you're in a syndicate.

Consider the IT worker in New York who in 2011 passed on the office lottery pool one week – the same week that his colleagues won a $319 million jackpot, meaning he missed out on a $16 million lump sum share of the total. He must be kicking himself now. None of us wants to feel that same way. So if someone were to offer to buy our tickets from us, it's unlikely that many of us would agree.

PAYING TO DREAM

It would be hypocritical to suggest that no one should ever buy lottery tickets, because I myself like to buy a ticket every now and again.

On the one hand, there are many reasons why it is a bad idea. Depending on the lottery, the odds are so infinitesimally small that, with a clear head, it is laughable to think there is any point in purchasing a ticket. Learning the odds that you'll win is a boring detail that takes some of the buzz out of buying the ticket, but it might help to reinforce the thought that you are almost certainly not going to win.

And if you *do* win, it's not clear that the change in lifestyle would actually have a persistent long-term effect on your happiness levels. As explored in Lesson 3, we tend to expect that a single event will have an outsized effect on our future happiness, ignoring the many other factors that will be vying for our attention.

Instead of spending £2 on a weekly ticket, you could automatically transfer it into a savings account. Even assuming a 0% interest rate, at the end of the year this £104 could be a treat — not a seven-hundred-million-dollar life-changing treat, admittedly, but something fun nonetheless. Keep it in an account to roll it into the next year, and assume a 1% compound interest, and over 15 years this will amount to £1,674. Stick it into a higher performing index fund with average returns of 7% and it could be £2,613. Of course you will have to consider taxes, fees and the impact of inflation, but it still might be your preferred choice over using this money on the lottery.

On the other hand, as long as the amount you are paying is low enough that it doesn't harm your financial position, it could be thought of as the price to pay for the comfort of avoiding regret and the joy of dreaming. You have to be in it to win it.

TRUST AND LONG-TERM MINDSETS

Which is better: a bird in the hand or two in the bush? What about one marshmallow now or two later?

The ability to forgo immediate pleasure for a larger return later is a keystone of many of the biggest challenges in all areas of our lives. We need to invest now – whether that means giving up spending, calories, comfort, TV time – to reap some benefits in the future.

This future-oriented behaviour has traditionally been thought of as the result of exerting self-control (see Lesson 19). In a now-classic study, psychologist Walter Mischel's research team gave children one marshmallow (or other treat) and explained that they could eat that one now or could wait for two later. Some children try to resist the sugary deliciousness while others succumb to temptation.

In follow-up studies, this ability to delay gratification was found to be linked to positive outcomes later in life. Those children who held out for two treats tended to fare better down the line, from wealth to education to lower crime rates and lower substance misuse. So, understandably, researchers have been trying to decode the secrets of self-control to unlock these future benefits. But it turns out that self-control is only part of the equation.

What if you aren't sure that the future reward, the two marshmallows, will ever materialize? Then the question becomes not whether to indulge in a small reward now or a larger reward later, but something rather different: whether to indulge now with certainty or to have the 'possibility' of something later?

Celeste Kidd and colleagues set out to test this by modifying the marshmallow experiment. In the modification, the researchers first engaged the youngsters in a decoy task – to decorate a piece of paper with the mediocre art supplies that were on the table. All of the children were told that if they hung on a little while, the adult would go get some better craft supplies for them. Here's where the experiment starts. For half of the kids, the researcher did indeed return with the better art supplies; this was to demonstrate reliability. Conversely, for the other half, the researcher returned empty-handed, apologizing to the child and saying that they were mistaken; this of course demonstrates unreliability. All children were then offered the marshmallow trade-off of one now or two later.

The results are insightful. The children who experienced unreliability waited on average just over 3 minutes before eating the marshmallow, and only 1 of the 14 kids waited the full time to receive the larger treat. On the other hand, of the children who had reliably received the better art supplies, the average waiting time for the group was around 12 minutes, and a whopping 9 out of 14 held out for the two marshmallows. This shows that self-control is not the only determining factor of whether they held out for a larger reward later. Trust that the researcher would make good on her promise dramatically influenced how the children responded to the challenge.

So the answer to whether a bird in the hand is better than two in the bush depends partly on your confidence that the birds will still be there by the time you reach it.

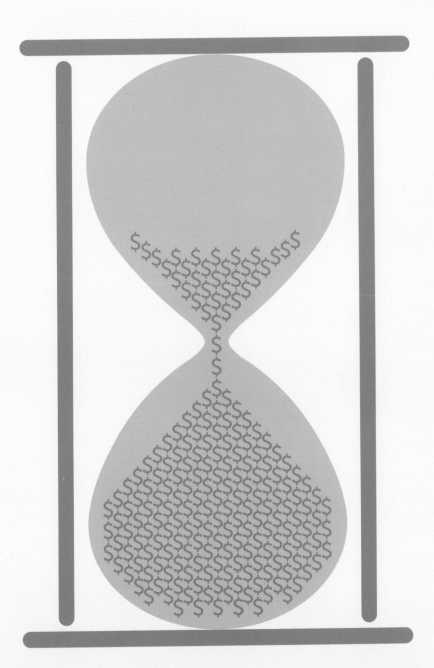

BUILDING TRUST

This new twist on the research should perhaps not be surprising. When we think about our daily interactions, it is clear that we place trust in strangers every time we hand over money to buy something. You have to trust that the money you give to the barista will result in a triple soy latte. This research shows that trust becomes even more important when the return (the cup of coffee) is not immediate but is promised sometime later.

For us to deem future-oriented behaviour to be in our best interest, the people, companies, employers and governments with whom we interact must be worthy of our trust, and the situation needs to be reliable enough that we can be confident that promises of a better outcome in the future will actually be delivered.

This also highlights the vicious cycle that financial fragility can create. Not having enough money to make ends meet can accentuate unreliability and instability, which in turn promotes short-termism and hinders the inclination to plan for the long term. If it is difficult to pay rent each month and there is a threat of eviction, how does this unreliability and instability affect our choices?

In an age of pushing for quarterly results, short-term objectives and revolving political cycles, long-term planning can be undermined. However, it is paramount for financial institutions and even governments to build trust and instil confidence in the reliability of their systems. In this regard, the practice of many banks guaranteeing a certain level of funds ($250,000 in USA, $250,000 in Australia, £85,000 in UK) does help to ensure a minimum level of reliability. Alongside this, financial institutions would do well to have adequate transparency to reassure people that they are always working in the service of their customers.

While the onus is on the institutions with which we interact to instil in us a sense of trust, there may be things that we can do to help ourselves to make decisions that are in our own best interest.

One is to try to understand realistic timeframes. Even though some rewards will be uncertain in size and timeframe, having a better understanding of the likely return may help to prevent the feeling of doubt that it will materialize, and may help maintain the stamina needed to continue waiting.

To encourage or facilitate our kids', colleagues' or family's long-term 'investment' behaviour, we should do what we can to create an environment that they can rely upon, and deliver on promises of things to come.

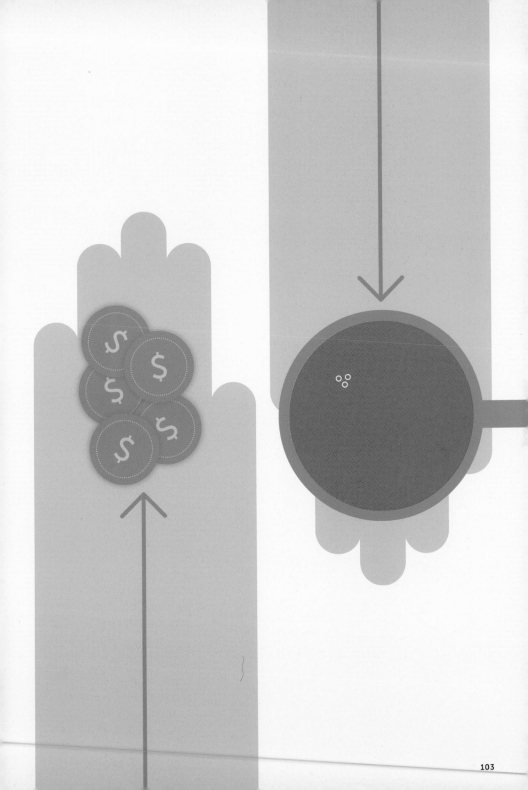

HOW WILL
YOUR FUTU

YOU FUND
RE?

WHY IS IT SO DIFFICULT TO PREPARE FOR THE FUTURE?

Financial wellbeing is a lot like health. And if you've ever skipped a spinning class to lie on the sofa with a glass of wine and a bad TV programme, you'll appreciate that while physical health is a goal we know we *should* strive for, it is not always easy to convince ourselves that we *want* to take the steps to achieve that goal. Similarly, financial health often requires immediate sacrifices to gain unknown benefits in the future.

This is perhaps why it can be so unappealing to plan for the future. As we've seen in other lessons, humans care more about 'now' than 'later'. Building a financially healthy future requires sacrifices now, incurring the immediate 'cost' of effort to sit down to make a plan, and the recurring 'costs' of giving up some spending today for a more comfortable life later.

When we're relatively young, most of our important financial milestones are in the future and full of questions – what will the world be like? What will my expenses be at that time? Who else will depend on me financially? Where will I be living? At what age will I stop working? Will I have saved enough to retire comfortably? And in some ways it feels as though it won't really be happening to *me*, but rather to

an older, future version of me. That events such as buying a house or retirement can feel so distant on all of these dimensions – temporally (it's in the future), socially (it's not happening to me, it's happening to my future-self), and hypothetically (it's uncertain what it will entail) – helps to explain why it can be difficult to plan accordingly.

If we look to the horizon we may see the blur of a few shapes, but if we look under a microscope we can see with great detail. In the same way, when events are psychologically distant, we tend to think of them in a more abstract way. And the more abstract the event, the less compelled we are to take action.

Conversely, when events are psychologically close – that is, when they are happening to me right now, right here – we tend to think of them in more concrete terms, with more detail. This concrete construal of the event is much more conducive to making and acting upon plans.

We weigh up costs and benefits all the time. In the case of forward planning, the fact that the costs of funding our future lifestyle and retirement are immediate and clear, yet the benefits are in the future and unclear, tips the balance in favour of inertia.

When events are psychologically distant, we tend to think of them in a more abstract way.

When events are psychologically close, we tend to think of them in more concrete terms, with more detail.

CONNECT WITH YOUR FUTURE SELF

Given this construal level theory, in which events that are psychologically distant are also construed at a more abstract and less compelling level, what can we do to help ourselves feel more inclined to financially prepare for our future?

As a start, we could bring the distant to the here and now.

By increasing the vividness of our potential future, we can bridge the gap in empathy between our current self and our future self. In one experiment, Hal Hershfield and colleagues asked people to indicate how much they would like to contribute to their retirement fund by moving a slider along the computer screen. As the person moved the slider, a photo of them either smiled or frowned depending on the amount selected.

For half of the participants, their image smiled when less money was committed to the retirement fund, because more money could be used in the present day. But for the other half, their image was digitally enhanced to look like their 65-year-old future selves – grey hair and all – and thus smiled when people chose to contribute more to their retirement fund. The researchers found that people who saw their aged image chose to contribute significantly more to their future than those who saw their present-day image.

In a related study, researchers explored how our perceptions of our future selves relate to our choices about pension contributions. They found that if people feel a sense of connection with their future self, and are reminded of their moral obligation to look after their future self, they are likely to save more (than if they were simply reminded of the effect on their own wellbeing in the future). However, for people who don't feel very connected, there is no discernible difference in the two types of messaging on savings rates for the future.

Therefore good practice may be to both make yourself feel more connected to your future self, whether that takes an aged selfie, a letter to yourself or visualizing your future retirement-age purchases, and then remind yourself of the responsibility you have now to look after that person in the future. As summarized by behavioural scientist Dan Ariely and co-author Jeff Kreisler, 'the more we can make the future defined, vivid, and detailed, the more relatable it becomes, and the more we'll care, connect, and act in our future selves' interests, too'.

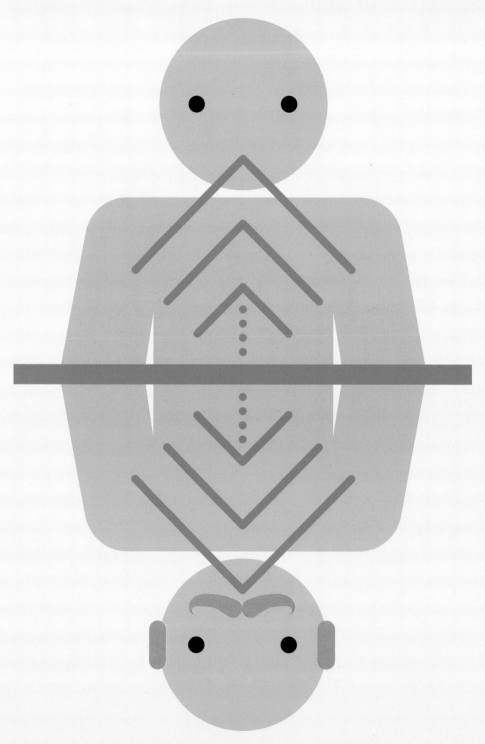

RETIREMENT READY?

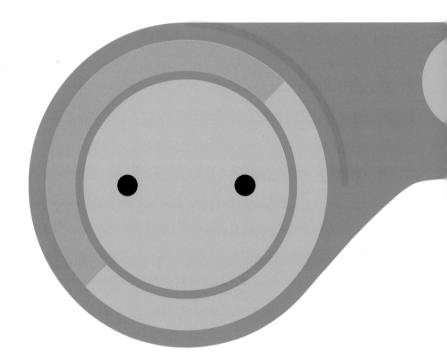

Admittedly, the topic of financial planning for retirement sounds endlessly boring. But in some ways it is totally intriguing, because despite the relatively high stakes (who wants to be destitute at 80?), many of us seem to be utterly unmoved to do much about it. On the surface, retirement planning should be easy: we all know that it is in our own best interest to save for retirement. Yet few people attempt to make a plan, and even fewer stick to that plan. Why?

In extreme cases, some people simply do not have any slack in their day-to-day finances to be able to save for retirement. Yet many people who do have slack are also failing to adequately prepare.

Researchers Annamaria Lusardi and Olivia Mitchell found that only 31% of the Americans they surveyed had even *tried* to make a retirement plan, and people who were less familiar with financial concepts such as inflation, interest and risk were less likely to have tried than people who were more familiar with them. Of that 31%, only about two-thirds actually developed a plan, and fewer still stuck to it. Overall, the

researchers found that only about 1 in 5 people successfully followed a plan.

There are many reasons why even contemplating doing the planning may be hard. In Lesson 15 we discussed how things that seem psychologically distant are less compelling for us to act upon. Saving for retirement feels distant along many dimensions. Additionally, financial literacy is scarce, so for many of us it isn't really clear what to do. And the benefits accrue only in the future, not to me but to my 'future self', making retirement planning even harder to

imagine. It is no wonder then that inertia is so powerful.

Even if you muster up the energy to make a retirement plan, sticking with it can be challenging. An unexpected expense might crop up, thwarting good intentions to put money aside. And saving requires some degree of self-control; we must forgo current spending right now, today, for a likely but not certain future benefit. Harassing yourself on a month-to-month, or purchase-to-purchase basis to save for retirement would be tiring and sap anyone's willpower.

ALL SYSTEMS GO

Rather than, or in addition to, us relying on willpower, there are ways in which the process of saving can be designed to reduce our effort.

Some countries take the effort out of planning for retirement by having mandatory pension plans. In Australia, for example, employers must pay 9.5% of your salary into a pension for you for when you retire. While this may feel too heavy-handed for some readers, for others it may be a welcome helping hand.

In other countries, for example in the UK, a minimum pension contribution is now the default, meaning that employers must offer a pension plan and automatically enrol new employees into the plan, unless or until the employee chooses to leave the plan. Redesigning the system so that people have to actively opt out harnesses the power of inertia: no effort is required to stay in the plan, in fact it would take some effort to *not* save for your retirement.

The methods above, either mandating pensions or auto-enrolling workers into them, also remove at least some of the dependency on financial literacy and numeracy. That is, these approaches do not rely on you being a financial whiz. Those who love maths and those who don't have equally good potential shots at saving effectively.

While these approaches have been found to encourage people to start contributing to their pension, there is an important caveat: the actual percentage that best suits you might be different to the default rate. So before patting yourself on the back for being nudged into contributing to your future, check that the rate is appropriate for you, and consider topping it up with additional contributions that fit within your budget.

A difficulty here is that there is little to no opportunity to learn whether our choices have been bad or good. Some of our biggest (highest stakes) events are those that happen only once, or maybe a few times, or maybe never, in our lives: buying a house, vocational or educational training, marriage and retirement. By the time we know whether we have chosen sub-optimally, it may be too late to fix. It will be a value judgement for each person, but given how many of us are inadequately prepared, and knowing how easily we can adapt to our current situation, it seems that the best bet would be to err on the side of caution and to boost our retirement savings.

Our employers can help us to help ourselves in other ways, too. Employers could allow, or even encourage, us to commit to increasing our contributions at the next pay rise. This helps because you make the decision upfront, before you have a chance to miss the money. People typically dislike losses – more so than they like an equivalent gain. The auto-escalation approach to pension contributions minimizes this loss aversion because, instead of a loss, the commitment becomes a 'forgone gain'. In other words, with each pay rise, you may still have more money to spend than pre-pay rise, just not as much as you would have had had you not committed it. Therefore, you are less likely to feel that you are sacrificing present-day spending.

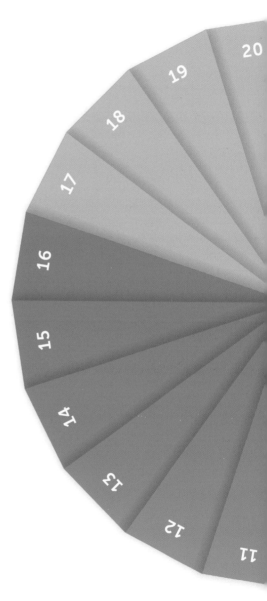

TOOLKIT

13

You're almost certainly not going to win the lottery. People generally overestimate their odds of winning, but the cost of a ticket might be worth it for the fun of imagining a different lifestyle or to avoid the regret you'd feel if you missed out on the office syndicate.

14

Short-termism is problematic for financial wellbeing. But short-termism isn't only about craving instant gratification or a lack of self-control, it also depends on your expectations about the future. Why delay your gratification if there is the chance that whatever you are holding out for might not materialize? This means that the reliability of a situation and how much we can trust others (people or institutions) is important for fostering future-oriented behaviour to improve long-term outcomes.

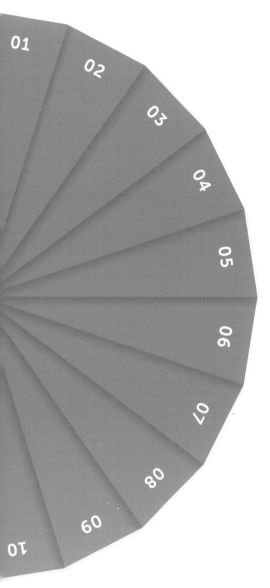

15

Retirement, and our future more generally, feels psychologically distant. At the same time, the requisite sacrifices to financially secure our future feel psychologically close. This mismatch – the costs are here and now while the benefits are unclear and in the future – is likely to dampen our motivation to make a plan. We can increase our motivation by morphing future, unclear benefits to immediate, clear benefits. To help yourself to save more, get in touch with your 'future self'.

16

Not enough people are prepared financially for retirement. With the upfront costs and delayed benefits of pensions, our present-bias makes giving up spending now to save for the future rather unattractive. The way that pensions are designed can help mitigate this reluctance. There are a number of measures that employers can take to make retirement planning easier, such as allowing us to pre-commit to escalating contributions. So ask your employer what they can do to help you prepare for the future.

FURTHER LEARNING

READ

Nudge: Improving decisions about health, wealth and happiness
Richard Thaler and Cass Sunstein
(Penguin, 2009)

Save more tomorrow™: Using behavioral economics to increase employee saving
Thaler, R. H., & Benartzi, S., *Journal of Political Economy*, 112(S1), S164-S187 (2004)

WATCH

The battle between your present and future self
Daniel Goldstein
TED Talk

We tested an economic theory by trying to buy people's Powerball tickets for much more than they paid
Business Insider test the concept of regret avoidance with lottery ticket holders
businessinsider.com.au

EXPLORE

The Marshmallow Study Revisited
Learn more about the marshmallow test revisited in an interview with the researchers and accompanying video
rochester.edu/news

DO

(Digitally) age yourself
Download an app that transforms photos; seeing an aged version of yourself may help build empathy with your future self.

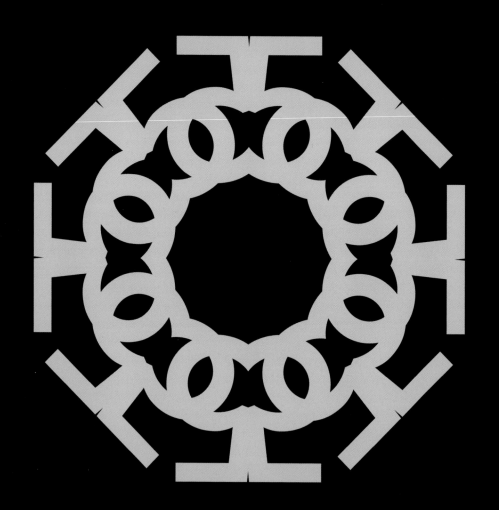

BETTER WITH MONEY

LESSONS

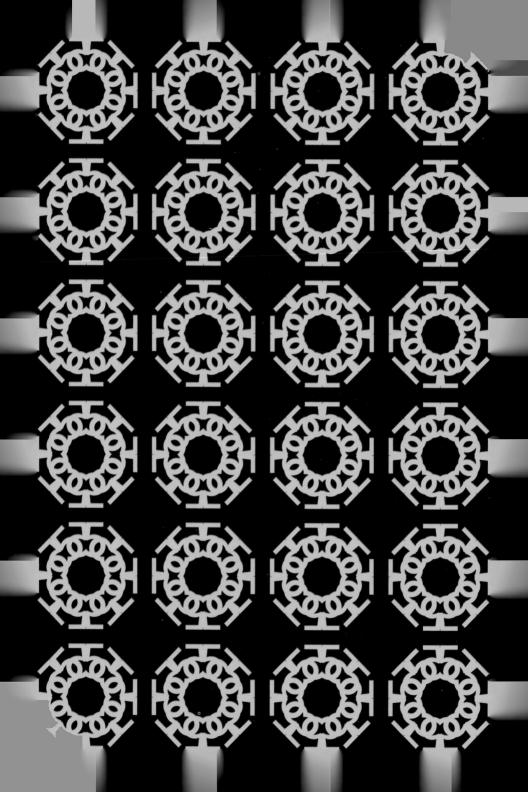

While we know that having money doesn't make us happy per se, it does provide opportunities for valuable experiences.

In the previous three sections we learned that the key components to financial wellbeing are to make ends meet to cover the basics; to build a buffer in order to be resilient to shocks; and to think beyond today to plan for the long term.

Easier said than done, perhaps. So in this section we will explore how goal-setting could be used to help work towards these aims, the role of willpower in this ambition and some techniques that may help us stick the course.

With all these good intentions and new strategies, it may feel as if there are blue skies ahead, and it is worth considering what happens as we do start building financial wellbeing. Changes to lifestyle soon become the new normal as we adapt to our changed circumstances. The point is not to endlessly chase wealth only to acclimatize and seek out even more; it is to build some financial security because money opens up choices that may otherwise be unavailable.

Having some financial slack not only covers those rainy-day emergencies without resorting to expensive debt, it also allows us to pursue dreams beyond the basics of getting by. For example, money helps us to upskill or retrain to pursue a different career, or could be the start-up capital needed for that great business idea. When we're not stressed about money, it may make other areas of life feel more manageable too.

Financial wellbeing is not just about scrimping, saving and sacrificing. So what to do when you feel that you're in a comfortable place to spend? While we know that having money doesn't make you happy per se, it does provide opportunities for valuable experiences. So in this section we also explore the fun to be had spending it. After all, we all have to live a little!

CAN'T KEEP UP?

We humans are a resilient bunch, and pretty adaptable, too. This can be useful when something negative happens to us, but when we are hoping that something positive will bring us happiness, this adaptation can keep us always chasing for more.

When we get used to new circumstances, our point of reference changes. So going back to our original level of consumption would actually feel like a loss. And people don't like losses; in fact, we feel the pain of a loss more than we feel the pleasure of an equivalently sized gain, a concept called loss aversion.

Let's say you used to eat one ice cream cone per year. Your reference point would usually be zero, and your annual cone brings a big boost of happiness. Then an ice cream parlour opens up right next door to your home. Your ice cream consumption sky rockets to a cone per day. At first this is

wonderful, but then it becomes, well, just normal. And the day you don't have an ice cream, it feels like you are sacrificing a lot. Because a daily single scoop is your new normal, you plump for two scoops when you need a treat. And then once you have adapted to two scoops, you need hot fudge and a cone that is chocolate-dipped and rolled in nuts to move the dial from normal to indulgence. And so it continues . . .

Hedonic treadmill

The problem is an endless striving for more and more, just to try to maintain the level of extra happiness that we have become accustomed to. Psychologists call this the hedonic treadmill. This means that we may not be deriving as much longterm happiness from buying stuff as expected.

It is easy to compare ourselves with those who are seemingly financially better off than

us. This upward social comparison leads to a positional 'arms race', where we accumulate more and more stuff in an effort to elevate our position as compared with our friends and neighbours, and then they buy more stuff in order to elevate their own position relative to us. Economist Robert Frank explains that on an individual level, someone may feel better when they buy a more expensive car than their neighbour because they attain a higher unspoken status, but on a societal level it is a zero sum game. When one person leapfrogs another to gain higher rank, by necessity another person loses his place in rank, so overall as a society there is no improvement in happiness.

Of course, the extent to which we are vulnerable to the hedonic treadmill will depend somewhat on individual differences, our temperaments and the type of events that take place. In some cases, rather than adapting, we may even become sensitized; that is, a continuation of something can accentuate (rather than attenuate) the amount of pleasure or pain it brings.

The point here, however, is not to generate a mathematical formula for when and where the hedonic hit from a particular purchase will start to dissipate, rather it is to highlight that the happiness you have about a purchase is likely to be at its highest right at the start – there is a good chance that it will wear off after purchase as your reference point changes. Knowing this might raise the question about whether the purchase is really worth it. If you feel as though it is hard to keep up with even your own expectations, console yourself with the knowledge that you are not alone. The hedonic treadmill has many of us running just to stand still.

GETTING USED TO THE HIGH LIFE

What does all this talk of treadmills really tell us? It is another link between how and why we behave, and our relationship with money. If the hedonic treadmill means that we are constantly striving for more to fuel our upward adaptation, then there are a few lessons to be learned.

Will it get easier?

It can be tempting to put off certain financial tasks, such as paying down debt, saving for retirement, or working towards a deposit now in the expectation that it will be easier to do later on in life when you will potentially be earning more money. But this can leave you in a vulnerable position. First of all, there is no guarantee that you will earn more

later. And even if you do earn more at that indeterminate point in time in the future, when (if) you recognize it, you will probably have already grown accustomed to your standard of living, so putting money away into savings then will likely also be painful.

Realistic expectations

If we are on the treadmill, then to maintain a given state of happiness will require improving our circumstances over time. That may be done in many different ways, not just materially. But to the extent that you will want material improvements as well, this should be built into long-term plans. What this means practically is that if you spend £x this year, build more than £x into next year's budget.

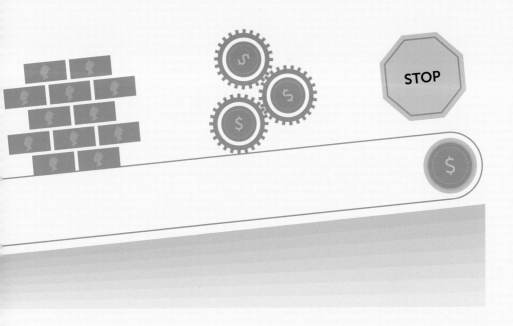

Slowing the treadmill

Another approach would be to try to step off the treadmill or at least slow it down. To do so, when we choose things or experiences, we can select those that we adapt less easily to. For example, novelty (it is new to you) and variability (it is different each time, like a gym class or a magazine subscription) seem to slow adaptation, and similarly, extending the length of time between a repeating event can help. When the ice cream cone is daily, it is mundane; when it is monthly, it becomes a treat.

So what *will* bring lasting happiness? There are hundreds of books, websites and organizations dedicated to this topic. Nurturing social connections, getting more exercise, finding meaning or purpose, and spending time appreciating nature are recurring themes.

Being financially healthy doesn't make any of these strategies magically happen. But with better financial wellbeing, the absence of the stress and strain of not having enough money can help us to focus on building these strategies into our lives.

The hedonic treadmill has many of us running just to stand still.

SETTING GOALS

Maybe it's buying a yacht. Maybe it's to retire at 50. Or maybe it's just to reach the end of the month without dipping into the overdraft. Most of us have financial goals, but their scope, scale and the extent to which they are clearly defined – even in our own minds – will vary from person to person.

When we set goals that are specific and somewhat difficult, we're likely to do better than if just following a more vague ambition to 'do our best'. Our commitment to a given goal depends on its value (how important it is to us), and how attainable the goal is.

Looking to the early retirement example, the goal might be made more specific by breaking it down to investing £x thousand per year. The value, or why it is important and matters to you, may be to escape the daily grind and devote yourself to wooden spoon carving.

How do we know how attainable the goal is? This will depend on how difficult it is. Too easy and it's boring; too difficult and it causes anxiety. It also depends on our self-efficacy – that is, our belief in our own capacity to do what we've set out to do.

Making sure that the goal is time-bound helps us to avoid slipping into inertia or procrastinating for too long. Getting feedback on our progress towards these ambitions is also crucial. After all, if we don't know whether we're on or off track, how can we correct our course?

With all this talk of goals it may be tempting to set yourself a stack of different goals all at once. However, behavioural scientist and University of Toronto professor Dilip Soman and colleagues have found that setting a single, clear goal can be more effective than setting many goals. The idea here is that when we try to complete a goal we have to first think about the goal itself and then consider how, exactly, to achieve that goal. In practice this might be the difference between thinking about a goal of saving £400 for a trip to Paris, and then thinking that how to do that will be to bring a packed lunch to work rather than buy food out. According to the research, setting multiple goals could result in us spending too much mental effort on the trade-off decision of which goal to work towards (such as saving for the much-needed holiday, for retirement or for a new car) that we fail to move to the next mindset where we determine how to do that.

GOLDILOCKS GOALS

Putting this into practice, a good bet is to create a financial goal that's 'just right' - the type that Goldilocks would choose if she happened upon it.

So, when setting financial goals, they should be specific, without drilling down too far into the detail that it creates a complex tiering of sub-goals. They should be difficult enough that they are worthwhile, but not so difficult that they feel unattainable. We should be able to receive just the right type of feedback that keeps us energized and on track, without making a little slip off track feel like a complete failure.

With a 'just right' goal, neither too easy nor too difficult, set, what should we keep in mind while working towards it? Research suggests that there may be some side-effects to look out for.

Keep our risk-taking in check

Setting a goal might change our point of reference – instead of thinking about life as it is now, we may start to think about how life will be when that goal is reached. If that is the case, then it can feel as though we are always in the 'loss domain', as economists would say. That is, we feel as if we are behind and trying to catch up with our goal. And when in the loss domain, people tend to take a few more risks than otherwise. So, when pursuing a goal, consider whether your behaviour is a bit riskier than usual and to what degree you are comfortable with that.

View actions as a commitment to the goal

Psychologists Ayelet Fishbach and Ravi Dhar explain that the way people interpret their actions towards the goal influences later behaviour. If, by taking an action, you feel you've made progress, this could possibly lead you to give yourself licence to coast, potentially ending up off course. To prevent this, it could be helpful to reframe your step closer as strengthening your original commitment to the goal rather than as strict progress.

Remember the big picture

It's possible to get too caught up in a goal, losing sight of the bigger picture. For example, by focusing too narrowly on a goal to save £100 per month, someone may resort to a payday loan to pay for an unexpected expense, which could be covered by the saving amount – an expensive choice when you compare the cost of borrowing to the very low interest earned on savings.

What else can help us stick to our Goldilocks goal? We've all seen the enthusiasm for New Year's resolutions wane by the time Valentine's Day rolls around. So in the next lesson, we'll dip into the science of willpower to uncover some techniques that may help us stick to our new, important, specific financial goals.

'GOOD' MON

JUST SAVIN

SPENDING

EY ISN'T
G, IT IS
WELL.

WILLPOWER

Willpower is a concept that on the one hand is so ordinary, yet on the other hand is so extraordinary. When it comes to money, the role of willpower is clear. At some point most of us will need to call upon our reserves of self-control to override impulses and temptation. What that temptation is may differ from person to person, and depend on your current financial situation.

For people who tend to be on the spendthrift end of the spectrum, resisting unnecessary spending is an obvious challenge. For others, willpower is needed to avoid being an ostrich (staying in comfortable ignorance of your actual financial position) or a meerkat (checking your stock performance too frequently). Willpower is needed both to sit down and draw up a financial management plan when you could be doing something more entertaining, and then to actually stick to it over time. At a more basic level, in the absence of other intrinsic motivation, willpower is needed to simply get to work to earn a wage.

How can we improve willpower? Some researchers argue that willpower is like a muscle – easily fatigued in the short term, but able to develop with practice in the long term. Others, like psychologist Carol Dweck and her colleagues, have found that whether or not willpower strengthens or depletes depends on what the person *believes* about the nature of willpower. When told that exerting willpower helps people build their capability, research participants do no worse on multiple tests of self-control. But when told that the first exertion of willpower will sap people of their stores, they subsequently do worse.

While some of the biggest names in psychology have been studying willpower for over half a century, it seems that there are still plenty of questions that remain unanswered. A life of too much willpower is probably a drag, but a life with too little may leave us feeling trapped by circumstances and in a position that we'd rather not be in. By developing the practice of self-control, it becomes a tool that we can choose to use, or not use, at a level that is right for us.

Training willpower

Creates a tool

For better financial practices

USING WILLPOWER TO GET THE BEST FROM OUR MONEY

One way to work with willpower effectively is to create, where possible, an environment with fewer temptations, so that you don't have to rely on it in the first place. Sometimes you can alter your environment, for example, by changing a savings account to have restricted access, or by creating an automatic transfer out of your account after payday.

But, of course, there will be times when you are faced with a new or an uncontrollable environment. In these cases there are a number of strategies we can use to help ourselves.

Use the trigger

'If-then' strategies can be useful to anticipate a tempting situation and pre-emptively find your way out of it. These 'if-then' strategies, sometimes called implementation intentions, use the temptation triggers and provide alternative courses of action. They are statements we create that set out how we plan to stick to our goal in a given tempting situation. For example, someone might say, 'If I see that a shop is having a 20% off sale, then I will remind myself that I don't need any new clothes right now, and cross the street (or close the browser).'

Temptation bundling

Often, willpower is needed when the benefits don't accrue until later. A future reward is less compelling than an immediate one. So one strategy is to bring rewards forward. Try restricting your favourite treat to when you make a transfer to pay down your credit card or into savings, for example. This temptation bundling ties the thing that you find difficult to do to some tempting, immediate reward.

Seeing is believing

Congratulate yourself on strengthening your willpower each time you use it. If, indeed, our reserve of willpower grows or shrinks based on whether we believe it will grow or shrink, as discussed earlier, then thinking it grows is clearly a winning strategy.

Show gratitude

Psychology professor David DeSteno claims that to aid willpower, we should practise gratitude and compassion. According to DeSteno, '[w]hen you are experiencing these emotions, self-control is no longer a battle, for they work not by squashing our desires for pleasure in the moment but by increasing how much we value the future'.

Cool and hot

Willpower guru Walter Mischel explains that one way to develop self-control is to 'cool the now; heat the later' – injecting some psychological distance between us and the immediate temptation, while making the future reward seem more compelling. To 'cool the now', anything we can do to make the immediate reward seem more abstract can help. To 'heat the later', keeping a vivid picture of the goal in mind makes the future seem psychologically closer to us.

Future benefits

Current benefits

SPENDING TO
IMPROVE HAPPINESS

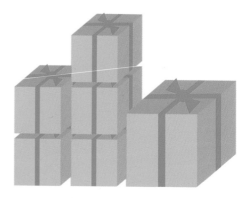

There has been a lot of emphasis in this book around the fact that money certainly cannot guarantee happiness. Nevertheless, it does give us options. It may feel like we all know how to spend – but do we know how to spend well? Research points to at least a few ways we can use our money to help boost happiness. The key here is that what matters is not how much you spend, but how you spend it.

Spend on others instead of yourself
Find some money on the ground? You may be happier spending it on someone else than on yourself. Elizabeth Dunn, a psychologist at University British Columbia, and her colleagues gave people either $5 or $20 and told half of them to spend it on themselves and the other half to spend it on someone else. When asked about their happiness at the end of the day, what mattered more than the amount of money was whether people had spent on others or themselves, with the former being the happier group.

It seems that who we give to also matters. According to Lara Aknin and others, spending on our close friends and family brings us more happiness than spending on acquaintances. Knowing the positive impact we've had also gives us a wellness boost. So when you receive a gift from someone, let them know the positive impact it has had on you.

Spend on experiences instead of things

Psychologists Leaf Van Boven and Tom Gilovich asked people to recall one material and one experiential purchase, and then asked which one brought more happiness: 57% responded that the experience made them happier, with only 34% indicating that the material purchase did. The reason may be that we adapt more slowly to experiences than to things, perhaps because we anticipate (look forward to) and mentally revisit (remember) them more. Essentially this means we get a bigger hedonic hit from experiences.

When asked about their happiness at the end of the day, what mattered was whether people had spent on others.

Spend on many small instead of one big

Would you prefer one long massage or two shorter ones? Researchers wanted to test whether breaking up an experience enhanced or diminished its enjoyment, so offered one 3-minute massage to some people and two shorter massages totalling 2 minutes 40 seconds to the others. By any standard, the first offer should seem objectively superior, and indeed most people believed that one long massage would be better. But when actually experiencing them, people rated the two shorter massages higher than the one long massage, and were willing to pay more for a massage cushion.

The concept of diminishing marginal return is useful here. Essentially, the more of something we have, the smaller the incremental addition to our happiness. An experience that is twice as long doesn't necessarily bring us twice the pleasure.

BIGGEST HAPPINESS BANG FOR YOUR BUCK

When we know more about our psychological inner workings, we can choose to spend in ways that work best for us. For example, since we know that we tend to adapt more slowly to many small purchases than one big purchase, simply spacing out some of our regular treats so that they feel less routine may make a difference. Here are some other tips.

Pre-paying allows us to enjoy the experience of consumption without any worries.

Spend to match your personality

While the tips above show increases in wellbeing on average across a group, other research finds that to really get the most from your spending, it should match your personality. Sandra Matz and others recruited participants who self-scored very high or very low on one of the 'Big Five' personality traits – extroversion. The researchers offered them a voucher to spend in either a highly extroverted way (at a pub) or in a highly introverted way (buying a book) and had them report back their happiness levels when they received the voucher, when they cashed in their voucher, and 30 minutes later. The extroverts were slightly happier in either case. The introverts reported an increase in happiness if using the book voucher, but, importantly, reported a decrease in happiness if using the pub voucher. This shows that when spending is mismatched to these fairly stable personality types, the boost to happiness may not exist, and in some cases mismatched spending may even be detrimental.

Buy yourself time

If you are time-poor, a great use of money is to buy yourself time. This may be by paying someone to help with household chores, cooking, shopping or any other errands that seem to be consuming your time and headspace.

Researchers gave working adults $40CND on two consecutive weekends. The study participants were randomly assigned either to spend on something that would save them time, or to spend on something material. Whatever they were assigned the first weekend was switched the next weekend. Each weekend, the person rated their overall happiness levels and their time-stress levels. People reported greater happiness (higher good mood and lower bad mood, and lower time stress) on their time-saving weekend, regardless of whether that came first or second.

Pre-pay: buy now and consume later

This is the opposite mantra to that of credit cards. Buying upfront and consuming later mitigates the pain of paying that we described in Lesson 6. You have already paid so can enjoy the experience of consumption without any worries about how or when you will be able to purchase the item. Additionally, pre-paying means you can look forward to the event. This anticipation is an added bonus to the actual consumption, and anticipation seems to have a stronger impact than simply reflecting on something, although both can bring joy.

**BUILD +
BECOME**

TOOLKIT

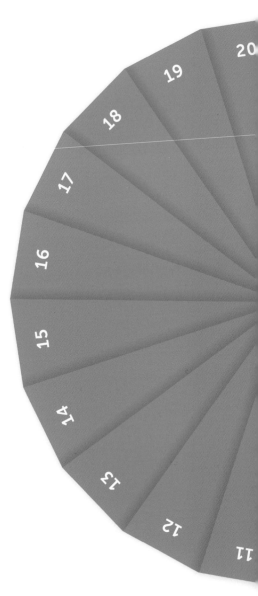

17

Humans are good at adapting, and it is easier to adjust to an upward change in our financial position than a downward change. This can be problematic when we approach our lives with the attitude of 'I'll pay off my debt/start saving for a deposit/put money away for retirement once I get paid more', because as soon as we do get paid more we start getting used to a better position and want to maintain it. This creates a constant pressure to strive for more just to maintain a given level of happiness.

18

Goal-setting can be helpful in working towards financial objectives. However, beware: some methods of setting goals are superior to others, and there can be some unintended consequences. Setting one specific and moderately difficult financial goal is a good start. It should be hard enough to be worth striving for, but not so hard that it feels unachievable.

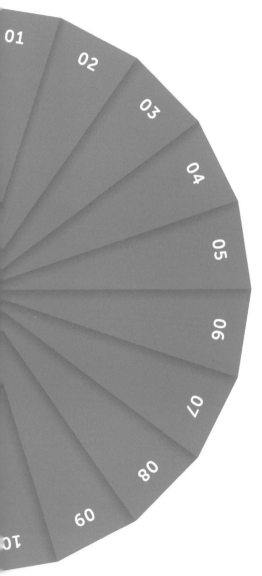

19

Willpower is a useful capability. One theory is that whether you think willpower depletes or strengthens with use affects whether it actually does. When confronted with a temptation, strategies such as 'if-then' plans, or psychologically distancing yourself from the immediate desire while bringing future rewards closer, may help. Alternatively, change your environment to avoid the temptation altogether.

20

How to get more happiness bang for your buck? Researchers find that spending on experiences (rather than things) and on others (not just yourself) brings higher wellbeing to people. Replace large infrequent purchases with smaller ones to mitigate adaptation. If you are time-poor, spending money to 'buy time' may boost happiness. Other tips include pre-paying for something and aligning your spending with your personality to get the most enjoyment.

FURTHER LEARNING

READ

If money doesn't make you happy, then you probably aren't spending it right
Dunn, E. W., Gilbert, D. T., & Wilson, T. D., *Journal of Consumer Psychology*, 21(2), 115-125 (2011)

How to Worry Less About Money
John Armstrong (School of Life, 2012)

The Marshmallow Test: Understanding self-control and how to master it
Waler Mischel (Bantam Press, 2014)

VISIT

stickK
Visit StickK.com if you have a commitment in mind that you need support sticking to.

Action for Happiness
Learn more and join the movement, especially if the hedonic treadmill is getting you down.
actionforhappiness.org

DO

Treat yourself
Pick a weekend to indulge and try out all of the tips from lesson 20.

EPILOGUE

Our relationship with money – the way we behave and the choices we make – is crucial to our financial wellbeing. These relationships are complex and the function of so many things, not least our own human psychology, the behaviour of others, the situations we find ourselves in, and our cultural and institutional frameworks.

For example, the power of social connections is such that even if we are not consciously seeking out advice from a friend, their choice of car – a Ferrari or Ford Fiesta, for example – affects our financial decisions whether we realize it or not. The policies of the country we live in will determine wage levels, costs of living and the shape of our retirement. Cultural values and previous experience will affect how we relate to money and financial priorities.

While it is worth developing a sense of control over our financial situation, our personal agency is not a magic wand. There are some things that we cannot change. Sometimes, even with the best intentions and a lot of effort, things go awry. So while we should all be striving for financial wellbeing, there is a balance to be found between recognizing the constraints of luck and context, and appreciating the effort we put in and the choices we make to improve our position, given the situation in which we live.

We should honour the balance inherent within the concept of financial wellbeing. We may make plans about how to use money while we're cool, calm and collected, but actually use it – spend it – in the heat of the moment. These controlled cold states and impulsive hot states don't always align,

While we should all be striving for financial wellbeing, there is a balance to be found between recognizing the constraints of luck and context, and appreciating the effort we put in and the choices we make to improve our position.

but we can honour both, by, for example, allowing ourselves to set commitment devices to keep us on track with savings goals, while also indulging guilt-free in a spontaneous opportunity to visit a friend.

Being good with money is neither being caught up in unsustainable consumption and frivolity, nor being resigned to severe minimalism and frugality. Having good money practices means making and sticking to plans to the extent that they serve us well, with enough slack in the system to be able to cope with, or even enjoy, unexpected turns in the road.

Understanding some of the weird, worrisome and wonderful ways we are with money, as explored in this book, may help on the journey towards financial wellbeing and being good with money.

BIBLIOGRAPHY

INTRODUCTION AND CHAPTER 1
References and Further Reading

Brickman, P., Coates, D., & Janoff-Bulman, R., 'Lottery winners and accident victims: Is happiness relative?', *Journal of Personality and Social Psychology*, 36(8), 917 (1978)

Confer, J. C., Easton, J. A., Fleischman, D. S., Goetz, C. D., Lewis, D. M., Perilloux, C., & Buss, D. M., 'Evolutionary psychology: Controversies, questions, prospects, and limitations', *American Psychologist*, 65(2), 110 (2010)

Frey, B. S., & Oberholzer-Gee, F., 'The cost of price incentives: An empirical analysis of motivation crowding-out', *The American Economic Review*, 87(4), 746–755 (1997)

Gilbert, D., & Wilson, T. "Miswanting: Some problems in the forecasting of future affective states" in *Thinking and feeling: The role of affect in social cognition*, edited by Joseph P. Forgas, 178–197, Cambridge University Press (2000)

Gneezy, U., & Rustichini, A., 'A fine is a price', *The Journal of Legal Studies*, 29(1), 1–17 (2000a)

Gneezy, U., & Rustichini, A., 'Pay enough or don't pay at all', *The Quarterly Journal of Economics*, 115(3), 791–810 (2000b)

Gneezy, U., & List, J. A., 'Putting behavioral economics to work: Testing for gift exchange in labor markets using field experiments', *Econometrica*, 74(5), 1365–1384 (2006)

Griskevicius, V., Ackerman, J. M., Cantú, S. M., Delton, A. W., Robertson, T. E., Simpson, J. A., Thompson, M.E., & Tybur, J. M., 'When the economy falters, do people spend or save? Responses to resource scarcity depend on childhood environments', *Psychological Science*, 24(2), 197–205 (2013)

Griskevicius, V., Redden, J. P., & Ackerman, J. M., 'The Fundamental Motives for Why We Buy', *The Interdisciplinary Science of Consumption*, 33 (2014)

Helliwell, J., Layard, R., & Sachs, J., *World Happiness Report 2017* (2017): www.worldhappiness.report

ING International Survey, 'Savings 2017' (2017): www.ezonomics.com/ing_international_surveys/savings-2017/

Kenrick, D. T., & Griskevicius, V., *The Rational Animal: How evolution made us smarter than we think*, Basic Books (2013)

Furnham A., Wilson E., Telford K., 'The meaning of money: The validation of a short money-types measure', *Personality and Individual Differences*, 52.6, 707–711 (2012)

Mead, N L., et al. 'Social exclusion causes people to spend and consume strategically in the service of affiliation,' *Journal of Consumer Research* 37.5, 902–919 (2010). Referenced in Kenrick & Griskevicius (2013).

Rick, S. I., Cryder, C. E. & Loewenstein, G., 'Tightwads and spendthrifts', *Journal of Consumer Research*, 34(6), 767–782 (2008)

Rick, S. I., Small, D. A. & Finkel, E. J., 'Fatal (fiscal) attraction: Spendthrifts and tightwads in marriage', *Journal of Marketing Research*, 48(2), 228–237 (2011)

Rick, S. I., 'Chapter 8: Tightwads, Spendthrifts, and the Pain of Paying: New Insights and Open Questions', in *The Interdisciplinary Science of Consumption*, edited by Preston, S. D, Kringelbach, M. L., Knutson, B., 147–159, MIT Press (2014)

Sandel, M. J., *What Money Can't Buy: the moral limits of markets*, Macmillan (2012)

Spencer, N., 'Hands up if you're an emotional shopper' (2013): www.ezonomics.com/stories/hands_up_if_youre_an_emotional_shopper/

Von Stumm, S., O'Creevy, M. F., & Furnham, A., 'Financial capability, money attitudes and socioeconomic status: Risks for experiencing adverse financial events', *Personality and Individual Differences*, 54(3), 344–349 (2013)

Wilson, T. D., Wheatley, T., Meyers, J. M., Gilbert, D. T., & Axsom, D., 'Focalism: A source of durability bias in affective forecasting', *Journal of personality and social psychology*, 78(5), 821 (2000)

Wilson, T. D., and Gilbert D. T., 'Affective forecasting: Knowing what to want,' *Current Directions in Psychological Science*, 14.3, 131–134 (2005)

CHAPTER 2
References and Further Reading

Ariely, D., 'The Pain of Paying: The Psychology of Money' (2013): www.youtube.com/watch?v=PCujWv7Mc8o

Ariely, D., *Predictably Irrational*, chapters 1 and 2, Harper Collins (2008)

Ariely, D., Loewenstein, G., & Prelec, D. '"Coherent arbitrariness": Stable demand curves without stable preferences,' *The Quarterly Journal of Economics*, 118(1), 73–106 (2003)

Brykman S., 'Resistance is useful! UI/UX case study: the indelicate art of friction' (2016): www.propelics.com/ui-friction/

Caldwell, L., *The Psychology of Price*, Crimson Publishing (2012)

Di Muro, F., & Noseworthy, T. J., 'Money isn't everything, but it helps if it doesn't look used: How the physical appearance of money influences spending,' *Journal of Consumer Research*, 39.6, 1330–1342 (2012)

Duhigg, C., *The Power of Habit: Why we do what we do and how and how to change*, Random House (2013)

eZonomics, 'Why frictionless banking isn't right for everyone' (2017): www.ezonomics.com/blogs/why-frictionless-banking-isnt-right-for-everyone/

Gherzi, S., Egan, D., Stewart, N., Haisley, E., & Ayton, P., 'The meerkat effect: Personality and market returns affect investors' portfolio monitoring behaviour', *Journal of Economic Behavior & Organization*, 107, 512–526 (2014)

Henley J., 'Sweden leads the race to become cashless society' (2016): www.theguardian.com/business/2016/jun/04/sweden-cashless-society-cards-phone-apps-leading-europe

ING International Survey, 'Savings 2017' (2017): www.ezonomics.com/ing_international_surveys/savings-2017/

ING International Survey, 'Mobile Banking 2017 – Cashless Society' (2017): www.ezonomics.com/ing_international_surveys/mobile-banking-2017-cashless-society/

Kahneman D., *Thinking Fast and Slow*, Allen Lane (2011)

Karlsson, N., Loewenstein, G., & Seppi, D., 'The ostrich effect: Selective attention to information,' *Journal of Risk and Uncertainty*, 38(2), 95–115 (2009)

Knutson, B., Rick, S., Wimmer, G. E., Prelec, D., & Loewenstein, G., 'Neural predictors of purchases', *Neuron*, 53.1, 147–156. (2007)

Milkman, K. L., Minson, J. A., & Volpp, K. G., 'Holding the Hunger Games hostage at the gym: An evaluation of temptation bundling', *Management Science*, 60.2, 283–299 (2013)

Money Advice Service, 'Money lives' (2014): www.moneyadviceservice.org.uk/en/corporate/money-lives

Murray, N., Holkar, M., & Mackenzie, P., 'In Control' (2016): www.moneyandmentalhealth.org/shopping-addiction

Olafsson, A., & Pagel, M., 'The ostrich in us: Selective attention to financial accounts, income, spending, and liquidity', *National Bureau of Economic Research Working Papers*, 23945, (2017)

Reynolds, E., 'Could adding friction to spending improve people's mental health?' (2017): www.theguardian.com/technology/2017/feb/04/tech-banking-mental-health-anxiety-bipolar-disorder

RSA, 'Student Design Award Winners' (2017): www.thersa.org/discover/publications-and-articles/rsa-blogs/2017/06/designing-our-futures-announcing-the-2017-rsa-student-design-award-winners

RSA, 'Student Design Award Winners' (2016): www.thersa.org/action-and-research/rsa-projects/design/student-design-awards/winners/winners-2016-2. Design: Max Pyuman, University of Nottingham

Ruberton, P. M., Gladstone, J., & Lyubomirsky, S. 'How your bank balance buys happiness: The importance of "cash on hand" to life satisfaction', *Emotion*, 16.5, 575 (2016)

Shiv, B., Carmon, Z., & Ariely, D., 'Placebo effects of marketing actions: Consumers may get what they pay for,' *Journal of Marketing Research*, 42.4, 383–393 (2005)

Sicherman, N., Loewenstein, G., Seppi, D. J., & Utkus, S. P., 'Financial attention', *The Review of Financial Studies*, 29(4), 863–897 (2015)

Soman, D., 'Effects of payment mechanism on spending behavior: The role of rehearsal and immediacy of payments', *Journal of Consumer Research*, 27.4, 460–474 (2001)

CHAPTER 3
References and Further Reading

Amar, M., Ariely, D., Ayal, S., Cryder, C. E., & Rick, S. I., 'Winning the battle but losing the war: The psychology of debt management', *Journal of Marketing Research*, 48(SPL), S38–S50 (2011)

Berman, J. Z., Tran, A. T., Lynch Jr, J. G., & Zauberman, G., 'Expense Neglect in Forecasting Personal Finances', *Journal of Marketing Research*, 53(4), 535–550 (2016)

Davidai, S., & Gilovich, T., 'The headwinds/tailwinds asymmetry: An availability bias in assessments of barriers and blessings', *Journal of Personality and Social Psychology*, 111.6, 835 (2016)

Frank, R., *Success and Luck: the myth of meritocracy*, Princeton University Press (2016)

Gathergood, J., & Weber, J., 'Self-control, financial literacy & the co-holding puzzle', *Journal of Economic Behavior & Organization*, 107, 455–469 (2014)

Gathergood, J., Mahoney, N., Stewart, N., & Weber, J. 'How Do Individuals Repay Their Debt? The Balance-Matching Heuristic', *National Bureau of Economic Research Working Papers*, 24161 (2017)

Hammond, C., *Mind Over Money: The psychology of money and how to use it better*, Canongate Books (2016)

Huo, Y. Research cited in Frank (2016).

Kahneman D., *Thinking Fast and Slow*, Allen Lane (2011)

Lewis, M., 'Obama's Way' (2012): www.vanityfair.com/news/2012/10/michael-lewis-profile-barack-obama

Loewenstein, G., Bryce, C., Hagmann, D., & Rajpal, S., 'Warning: You are about to be nudged', *Behavioral Science & Policy*, 1(1), 35–42 (2015)

Mani, A., Mullainathan, S., Shafir, E., & Zhao, J., 'Poverty impedes cognitive function', *Science*, 341(6149), 976–980 (2013)

McHugh, S., & Ranyard, R., 'Consumers' credit card repayment decisions: The role of higher anchors and future repayment concern', *Journal of Economic Psychology*, 52, 102–114 (2016)

Mischel, W., *The Marshmallow Test: understanding self-control and how to master it*, Random House (2014)

Mullainathan, S., & Shafir, E., *Scarcity: Why having too little means so much*, Macmillan (2013)

Puri, M., & Robinson, D. T., 'Optimism and economic choice', *Journal of Financial Economics*, 86(1), 71–99 (2007)

Sharot, T., 'The optimism bias', *Current Biology*, 21(23), R941–R945 (2011)

Shephard, D. D., Contreras, J. M., Meuris, J., te Kaat, A., Bailey, S., Custers, A., & Spencer, N., 'Beyond Financial Literacy' (2017) think.ing.com/uploads/reports/Beyond-financial-literacy_The-psychological-dimensions-of-financial-capability_Summary-paper.pdf

Stewart, N., 'The cost of anchoring on credit-card minimum repayments', *Psychological Science*, 20(1), 39–41 (2009)

Sussman, A. B., & Alter, A. L. 'The exception is the rule: Underestimating and overspending on exceptional expenses', *Journal of Consumer Research*, 39(4), 800-814 (2012)

Telyukova, I. A., 'Household need for liquidity and the credit card debt puzzle', *Review of Economic Studies*, 80(3), 1148–1177 (2013)

Twigger R., *Micromastery*, Penguin (2017)

Vohs, K.D., 'The poor's poor mental power', *Science*, 341(6149), 969–970 (2013)

Waitley, D., 'Denis Waitley Quotes': www.brainyquote.com/quotes/denis_waitley_165018

CHAPTER 4
References and Further Reading

Ariely, D. & Kreisler J., *Dollars and Sense*, 228, HarperCollins (2017)

Andersen, T., Annear, S. & Sweeney, E., 'Lottery introduces woman who won $758.7m Powerball jackpot' (2017): www.bostonglobe.com/metro/2017/08/24/powerball-jackpot-won-single-massachusetts-ticket/pg9AyyG7Cl6bubZ3AIOS6I/story.html

Brickman, P., Coates, D., & Janoff-Bulman, R., 'Lottery winners and accident victims: Is happiness relative?', *Journal of Personality and Social Psychology*, 36(8), 917 (1978)

Bryan, C. J., & Hershfield, H. E., 'You owe it to yourself: Boosting retirement saving with a responsibility-based appeal', *Decision*, 1(S), 2 (2013)

Chiaramonte, P., 'Worker skips office mega pool, loses share of $319M' (2011): nypost.com/2011/03/30/worker-skips-office-mega-pool-loses-share-of-319m/

Choi, J. J., Laibson, D., Madrian, B. C., & Metrick, A., 'Defined contribution pensions: Plan rules, participant choices, and the path of least resistance', *Tax Policy and the Economy*, 16, 67–113 (2002)

FDIC, 'Understanding Deposit Insurance': www.fdic.gov/deposit/deposits/

FSCS, 'Banks/building societies': www.fscs.org.uk/what-we-cover/products/banks-building-societies/

Hagen, S., 'The marshmallow test revisited' (2012): rochester.edu/news/show.php?id=4622

Hershfield, H. E., Goldstein, D. G., Sharpe, W. F., Fox, J., Yeykelis, L., Carstensen, L. L., & Bailenson, J. N., 'Increasing saving behavior through age-progressed renderings of the future self', *Journal of Marketing Research*, 48(SPL), S23–S37 (2011)

Ivey, P., 'Eyes on the prize' (2017): www.homesandproperty.co.uk/property-news/woman-wins-845k-raffle-house-having-bought-just-40worth-of-2-tickets-a112936.html

Kahneman, D., Knetsch, J. L., & Thaler, R. H., 'Anomalies: The endowment effect, loss aversion, and status quo bias', *Journal of Economic Perspectives*, 5(1), 193–206 (1991)

Kahneman D., & Tversky A., 'Prospect theory: An analysis of decision under risk', *Handbook of the fundamentals of financial decision making: Part I.*, 99–127 (2013)

Kidd, C., Palmeri, H., & Aslin, R. N., 'Rational snacking: Young children's decision-making on the marshmallow task is moderated by beliefs about environmental reliability', *Cognition*, 126(1), 109-114 (2013)

Lusardi, A., & Mitchell, O. S. Financial literacy and planning: Implications for retirement wellbeing', *National Bureau of Economic Research Working Papers*, 17078 (2011)

Lyons Cole, L., 'People who bought a Powerball lottery ticket prove a basic truth about money' (2017): uk.businessinsider.com/powerball-ticket-how-you-view-money-2017-8?r=US&IR=T

Mischel, W., *The Marshmallow Test: understanding self-control and how to master it*, Random House (2014)

Moffitt, T. E., Arseneault, L., Belsky, D., Dickson, N., Hancox, R. J., Harrington, H., et al., 'A gradient of childhood self-control predicts health, wealth, and public safety', *Proceedings of the National Academy of Sciences*, 108(7), 2693–2698 (2011)

MoneySmart, 'Banking': www.moneysmart.gov.au/managing-your-money/banking

Ocbazghi, E., & Silverstein, S., 'We tested an economic theory' (2017): uk.businessinsider.com/powerball-tickets-winning-numbers-regret-avoidance-behavioral-economics-2017-8

Spencer N., 'When is the right time to eat stale doughnuts?' (2013): www.thersa.org/discover/publications-and-articles/rsa-blogs/2013/01/when-is-the-right-time-to-eat-stale-doughnuts

Thaler, R. H., & Benartzi, S., 'Save more tomorrow™: Using behavioral economics to increase employee saving', *Journal of Political Economy*, 112(S1), S164–S187 (2004)

Trope, Y., & Liberman, N., 'Construal-level theory of psychological distance', *Psychological Review*, 117(2), 440 (2010)

Van Gelder, J-L., Hershfield, H.E., & Nordgren, L. F., 'Vividness of the future self predicts delinquency', *Psychological Science*, 24.6, 974–980 (2013)

Weber, E. U., Johnson, E. J., Milch, K. F., Chang, H., Brodscholl, J. C., & Goldstein, D. G., 'Asymmetric discounting in intertemporal choice: A query-theory account', *Psychological Science*, 18.6, 516–523 (2007)

Zeelenberg, M., & Pieters, R., 'Consequences of regret aversion in real life: The case of the Dutch postcode lottery', *Organizational Behavior and Human Decision Processes*, 93(2), 155–168 (2004)

CHAPTER 5 AND EPILOGUE
References and Further Reading

Ariely, D., & Kreisler, J., *Dollars and Sense*, chapter 16, Harper Collins (2017)

Aknin, L. B., Dunn, E. W., Whillans, A. V., Grant, A. M., & Norton, M. I., 'Making a difference matters: Impact unlocks the emotional benefits of prosocial spending', *Journal of Economic Behavior & Organization*, 88, 90–95 (2013)

Aknin, L. B., Sandstrom, G. M., Dunn, E. W., & Norton, M. I., 'It's the recipient that counts: Spending money on strong social ties leads to greater happiness than spending on weak social ties', *PloS One*, 6(2), e17018 (2011)

DeSteno, D., 'The only way to keep your resolutions' (2017): mobile.nytimes.com/2017/12/29/opinion/sunday/the-only-way-to-keep-your-resolutions.html

Diener, E., Lucas, R. E., & Scollon, C. N., 'Beyond the hedonic treadmill: revising the adaptation theory of well-being', *American Psychologist*, 61(4), 305 (2006)

Dunn, E. W., Aknin, L. B., & Norton, M. I., 'Spending money on others promotes happiness', *Science*, 319 (5870), 1687–1688 (2008)

Dunn, E. W., Gilbert, D. T., & Wilson, T. D., 'If money doesn't make you happy, then you probably aren't spending it right', *Journal of Consumer Psychology*, 21.2, 115–125, (2011)

Fishbach, A., & Dhar, R., 'Goals as excuses or guides: The liberating effect of perceived goal progress on choice', *Journal of Consumer Research*, 32(3), 370–377 (2005)

Fishbach, A., & Touré-Tillery, M., 'Motives and Goals' in *Introduction to Psychology: The Full Noba Collection*, Diener Education Fund Publishers (2014)

Frank, R. H., *The Darwin Economy: Liberty, competition, and the common good*, Princeton University Press (2011)

Frederick, S., & Loewenstein, G., 'Hedonic Adaptation', in *Well-being: Foundations of Hedonic Psychology* by Kahneman D., Diener, E., & Schwarz, N., Russell Sage Foundation (1999)

Goleman, D., *Focus: The hidden driver of excellence*, chapter 8, Bloomsbury (2013)

Gollwitzer, P. M., & Sheeran, P., 'Implementation intentions and goal achievement: A meta-analysis of effects and processes', *Advances in Experimental Social Psychology*, 38, 69–119 (2006)

Heath, C., Larrick, R. P., & Wu, G., 'Goals as reference points', *Cognitive Psychology*, 38(1), 79–109 (1999)

Job, V., Dweck, C. S., & Walton, G. M., 'Ego depletion – Is it all in your head? Implicit theories about willpower affect self-regulation', *Psychological Science*, 21(11), 1686–1693 (2010)

Kuhn, Peter, Peter Kooreman, Adriaan Soetevent, and Arie Kapteyn. 'The Effects of Lottery Prizes on Winners and Their Neighbors: Evidence from the Dutch Postcode Lottery.' *American Economic Review*, 101 (5): 2226-47 (2011)

Locke, E. A., & Latham, G. P., 'Building a practically useful theory of goal setting and task motivation: A 35-year odyssey', *American Psychologist*, 57(9), 705 (2002)

Matz, S. C., Gladstone, J. J., & Stillwell, D., 'Money buys happiness when spending fits our personality,' *Psychological Science*, 27.5, 715–725 (2016)

Milkman, K. L., Minson, J. A., & Volpp, K. G., 'Holding the Hunger Games Hostage at the Gym: An evaluation of temptation bundling', *Management Science*, 60(2), 283–299 (2013)

Mischel, W., *The Marshmallow Test: understanding self-control and how to master it*, Random House (2014)

Moffitt, T. E., Arseneault, L., Belsky, D., Dickson, N., Hancox, R. J., Harrington, H., et al., 'A gradient of childhood self-control predicts health, wealth, and public safety', *Proceedings of the National Academy of Sciences*, 108(7), 2693–2698 (2011)

Nelson, L. D., & Meyvis, T., 'Interrupted Consumption: Disrupting adaptation to hedonic experiences', *Journal of Marketing Research*, 45(6), 654–664 (2008)

Soman, D., & Cheema, A., 'When goals are counterproductive: The effects of violation of a behavioral goal on subsequent performance', *Journal of Consumer Research*, 31(1), 52–62 (2004)

Soman, D., & Zhao, M., 'The Fewer, the Better: Number of Goals and Savings Behavior', *Advances in Consumer Research*; 39, 45–46 (2011)

Tu, Y., & Hsee, C. K., 'Consumer happiness derived from inherent preferences versus learned preferences', *Current Opinion in Psychology*, 10, 83–88 (2016)

Whillans, A. V., Dunn, E. W., Smeets, P., Bekkers, R., & Norton, M. I., 'Buying time promotes happiness', *Proceedings of the National Academy of Sciences*, 114 (32), 8523–8527 (2017)

Woolley, K., & Fishbach, A., 'Immediate rewards predict adherence to long-term goals', *Personality and Social Psychology Bulletin*, 43(2), 151–162 (2017)

At BUILD+BECOME we believe in building knowledge that helps you navigate your world.

Our books help you make sense of the changing world around you by taking you from concept to real-life application through 20 accessible lessons designed to make you think. Create your library of knowledge.

BUILD +
BECOME
www.buildbecome.com
buildbecome@quarto.com

@buildbecome
@QuartoExplores

Using a unique, visual approach, Gerald Lynch explains the most important tech developments of the modern world – examining their impact on society and how, ultimately, we can use technology to achieve our full potential.

From the driverless transport systems hitting our roads to the nanobots and artificial intelligence pushing human capabilities to their limits, in 20 dip-in lessons this book introduces the most exciting and important technological concepts of our age, helping you to better understand the world around you today, tomorrow and in the decades to come.

Gerald Lynch is a technology and science journalist, and is currently Senior Editor of technology website TechRadar. Previously Editor of websites Gizmodo UK and Tech Digest, he has also written for publications such as *Kotaku* and *Lifehacker*, and is a regular technology pundit for the BBC. Gerald was on the judging panel for the James Dyson Award. He lives with his wife in London.

GERALD LYNCH

BUILD + BECOME

GET TECHNOLOGY

BE IN THE KNOW.
UPGRADE YOUR FUTURE.

KNOW TECHNOLOGY TODAY, TO EQUIP YOURSELF FOR TOMORROW.

Using a unique, visual approach to explore philosophical concepts, Adam Ferner shows how philosophy is one of our best tools for responding to the challenges of the modern world.

From philosophical 'people skills' to ethical and moral questions about our lifestyle choices, philosophy teaches us to ask the right questions, even if it doesn't necessarily hold all the answers. With 20 dip-in lessons from history's great philosophers alongside today's most pioneering thinkers, this book will guide you to think deeply and differently.

Adam Ferner has worked in academic philosophy both in France and the UK – but it's philosophy *outside* the academy that he enjoys the most. In addition to his scholarly research, he writes regularly for *The Philosophers' Magazine*, works at the Royal Institute of Philosophy and teaches in schools and youth centres in London.

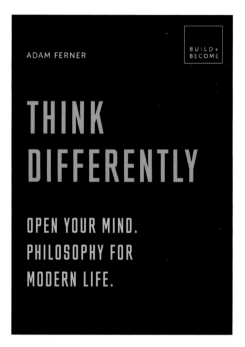

ADAM FERNER

BUILD + BECOME

THINK DIFFERENTLY

OPEN YOUR MIND. PHILOSOPHY FOR MODERN LIFE.

PHILOSOPHY IS ABOUT OUR LIVES AND HOW WE LIVE THEM.

Through a series of 20 practical and effective exercises, all using a unique visual approach, Michael Atavar challenges you to open your mind, shift your perspective and ignite your creativity. Whatever your passion, craft or aims, this book will expertly guide you from bright idea, through the tricky stages of development, to making your concepts a reality.

We often treat creativity as if it was something separate from us – in fact it is, as this book demonstrates, incredibly simple: creativity is nothing other than the very core of 'you'.

Michael Atavar is an artist and author. He has written four books on creativity – *How to Be an Artist, 12 Rules of Creativity, Everyone Is Creative* and *How to Have Creative Ideas in 24 Steps – Better Magic*. He also designed (with Miles Hanson) a set of creative cards *'210CARDS'*.

He works 1-2-1, runs workshops and gives talks about the impact of creativity on individuals and organizations. www.creativepractice.com

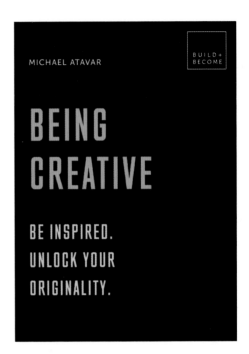

MICHAEL ATAVAR

BUILD + BECOME

BEING CREATIVE

BE INSPIRED. UNLOCK YOUR ORIGINALITY.

CREATIVITY BEGINS WITH YOU.

Using a unique, visual approach to explore the science of behaviour, *Read People* shows how understanding why people act in certain ways will make you more adept at communicating, more persuasive and a better judge of the motivations of others.

The increasing speed of communication in the modern world makes it more important than ever to understand the subtle behaviours behind everyday interactions. In 20 dip-in lessons, Rita Carter translates the signs that reveal a person's true feelings and intentions and exposes how these signals drive relationships, crowds and even society's behaviour. Learn the influencing tools used by leaders and recognize the fundamental patterns of behaviour that shape how we act and how we communicate.

Rita Carter is an award-winning medical and science writer, lecturer and broadcaster who specializes in the human brain: what it does, how it does it, and why. She is the author of *Mind Mapping* and has hosted a series of science lectures for public audience. Rita lives in the UK.

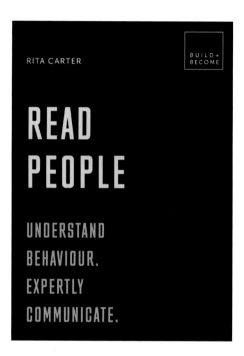

RITA CARTER

BUILD + BECOME

READ PEOPLE

UNDERSTAND
BEHAVIOUR.
EXPERTLY
COMMUNICATE.

CAN YOU SPOT A LIE?

We are living longer than ever and, thanks to technology, we are able to accomplish so much more. So why do we feel time poor? In 20 eye-opening lessons, Catherine Blyth combines cutting-edge science and psychology to show why time runs away from you, then provides the tools to get it back.

Learn why the clock speeds up just when you wish it would go slow, how your tempo can be manipulated and why we all misuse and miscalculate time. But you can beat the time thieves. Reset your body clock, refurbish your routine, harness momentum and slow down. Not only will time be more enjoyable, but you really will get more done.

Catherine Blyth is a writer, editor and broadcaster. Her books, including *The Art of Conversation* and *On Time*, have been published all over the world. She writes for publications including the *Daily Telegraph*, *Daily Mail* and *Observer* and presented *Why Does Happiness Write White?* for Radio 4. She lives in Oxford.

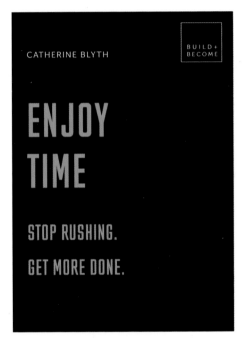

CATHERINE BLYTH

BUILD + BECOME

ENJOY TIME

STOP RUSHING.

GET MORE DONE.

TIME IS NOT MONEY.
TIME IS YOUR LIFE.

ACKNOWLEDGEMENTS

There are many people who helped bring this book to life. Special thanks to Lucy Warburton at White Lion Publishing for commissioning the book and Emma Harverson for project editing, Rachel Malig for copyediting and Stuart Tolley for the design work. Many thanks to everyone who read lessons, chapters, or even the whole book and provided feedback; any errors are mine. They are, alphabetically: Ian Bright, Jason Collins, Emily Daniels, Anne Lanjuin, Jeroen Nieboer, Scott Spencer, Juliette Tobias-Webb. Thank you to my colleagues, present and past, for the numerous and varied discussions about financial wellbeing, and to my family and friends for their encouragement and support. And finally, many thanks to my husband, Scott Spencer. Writing a book while starting a new job, moving house, and relocating across the globe is difficult; without him, it would have been impossible.

Nathalie Spencer is a behavioural scientist at Commonwealth Bank of Australia. She explores financial decision making and how insights from behavioural science can be used to boost financial wellbeing. Prior to CBA, Nathalie worked in London at ING where she wrote regularly for *eZonomics*, and at the RSA, where she co-authored *Wired for Imprudence: Behavioural Hurdles to Financial Capability*, among other titles. She has a Bachelor of Commerce from McGill University and a Master of Science in Behavioural Economics from Maastricht University. Born and raised in Boston USA, Nathalie has lived briefly in Canada, Germany, the Netherlands, and was based in the UK for over ten years before moving to Australia where she now lives.